Winning Strategies for Finding Exceptional Leaders
& Building a Sustainable Executive Recruiting Strategy

The
Executive
Recruiter's
Playbook

W.J. SHEWELOFF

Winning Strategies for Finding Exceptional Leaders
& Building a Sustainable Executive Recruiting Strategy

The
Executive
Recruiter's
Playbook

W.J. SHEWELOFF

THE EXECUTIVE RECRUITER'S PLAYBOOK

WINNING STRATEGIES FOR FINDING EXCEPTIONAL LEADERS & BUILDING A SUSTAINABLE EXECUTIVE RECRUITING STRATEGY

W. J. SHEWELOFF

CONTENTS

This book is dedicated to Harold C. "Mickey" McCray. He took me under his wing, nurtured me, and provided me with all the resources necessary for a long-term and successful career in retained executive search.
We worked together for over 30 years. Mickey passed away in 2022. I miss him dearly and remain forever grateful for his guidance and counsel over those years.

INTRODUCTION

With rare exceptions, 95% of Candidates I've successfully placed over my career were referred to me by Sources. Gaining referrals from Sources is one thing. Growing and nurturing a burgeoning referral base is another.

This book's objective is to help you execute and close searches with higher-quality Candidates and build the ideal referral base that will generate better-than-average referrals over time. Through a specific series of steps, I will help you improve your track record via the mindset and processes I've implemented while executing and honing each stage of a Search Methodology I've employed for over 30 years in the executive search business. This book will dive deep into sourcing, identifying, and recruiting strategies. Future volumes will explore critical aspects such as expectations, required skills, business development, reference checking, relocation challenges, and crafting compelling final offers. However, let me be clear: this is not a quick-fix guide. It's a long-term game, just like time-in-market and compounding in finance. If you're ready to invest time and effort to improve your craft and impact your career, this book is tailor-made for you. If you are willing to stretch your skills, this book will set you apart in the competitive world of talent acquisition.

With 35 years of experience in executive search, I've encountered numerous challenges and triumphed in the face of adversity. Throughout my career, I have successfully navigated complex situations, including assisting companies undergoing SEC investigations, rescuing failed search efforts initiated by other retained search firms, and exhibiting unwavering determination in sourcing highly qualified Candidates. Here are just a few examples to highlight my track record. In the appendix, you'll find a concise summary of the Search Methodology employed in these searches, presented in an easy-to-follow bullet-point format. Prepare to be inspired and equipped with invaluable insights for your search endeavors.

- I was called upon by the chairman of a life sciences company, who was preparing to terminate their chairman, chief executive officer, and chief financial officer. At the same time, they filed for voluntary bankruptcy and were de-listed from NASDAQ and required to re-state multiple previous quarterly statements. Understandably an ugly situation; however, I successfully placed both the chief executive officer and chief financial officer, after which the stock price increased by approximately 75%; the company moved out of bankruptcy and raised an additional $20 million through a rights offering. A couple of years later, I recruited a new board member who quickly became board chairman and helped sell the company at a profit.

- My searches performed for a southern California-based $120 million high technology client were compounded by their undergoing an SEC investigation brought about by prior management: Concurrent with the investigation, I identified and placed the CEO (where the search was completed in nine weeks, and the stock jumped 20%) and the CFO. I subsequently recruited their VP of global engineering. Additionally, we had three months to fill in the financial staff, and I successfully recruited and placed their director of treasury and risk management and director of external reporting. I completed these last three assignments concurrent with the company's planned relocation to the East Coast.

- In another instance, the chairman of the above-noted high technology client was chairman of a publicly held biotechnology company in Texas. He asked us to take over the search for a new president of the biotech firm he chaired after a nine-month failed recruitment effort by one of the top global search firms. I identified multiple qualified Candidates, including one highly skilled executive who had been approached by the previous search firm and turned them down. After turning me down three times, I encouraged him to pursue the opportunity, and he joined the firm, where he massively grew the business through tech innovation.

- While conducting a global search to identify a chief financial officer with a proven ability to raise $500 million before launching several communication satellites, I recruited an executive who backed out of the process twice. Despite this initial setback, I successfully re-engaged him. He eventually accepted a competitive offer to join the company.

- Another feather in my cap was collaborating closely with my partner over two years, placing approximately 75% of the senior management team in a privately held DOD satellite communications manufacturer, which grew tenfold during that same period. It was eventually sold at a significant profit.

- One of my proudest moments was managing the search for the president of a start-up company whose branded financial services product is still known today as CareCredit. After that successful search, I placed five more vice presidents and managers. Subsequently, the business was sold to General Electric, quickly becoming one of the most profitable business units. It's now a subsidiary of Synchrony Financial.

Every facet of an executive search is essential. However, this book will focus on my philosophy of building an ever-increasing referral base by encouraging Sources to refer qualified Prospects to me who agree to listen and learn about an opportunity. The primary goal is to create interest and intrigue about the role. Early in the conversation, I'll explore all matches against our client's required skill set. If I determine their qualifications meet or exceed the client's "Must Haves," then we'll discuss as much of the job as I can at that point in their candidacy and tailor it to address anything I've discovered might be of great interest as well as concern to this potential Candidate. When I had confidential searches, I would typically explore a Prospect's skill set first without revealing the title or name of the client. This is a slow dance, friends. Before assessing qualifications, gauge genuine interest in the job and willingness to share background information.

This book will assume the search agreement is already in force. You and other key executives of the recruiting team will meet with the client for the first time to learn more about the firm and what the client wants in the individual they choose to hire. We'll ensure that we walk away from the meeting(s) with solid insight into the client's culture, business goals, financials, current reason for the search, the behavioral style of the new hire's immediate manager as well as any executives involved in the hiring decision, and the primary duties of this Candidate. Then I'll take you step-by-step through my processes of sourcing, identifying, and ultimately recruiting excellent Candidates.

Below, I'll explain my mindset when performing searches and expanding my referral base. It has been the basis for my success in and enjoyment of this business. In the spirit of continuous learning, I have included an abbreviated history of executive search, how research tools have evolved, and definitions of frequently used terms.

PREFACE

MY PHILOSOPHY

Let's agree on one thing upfront: crucial to maintaining a successful relationship with your executive search client is your ability to consistently identify, recruit, and place the best talent available on each assignment, all within a reasonable amount of time.

This successful Candidate would have met most, if not all, of the requirements and expectations agreed upon with your client. And where they had limited experience, they made up for it in other areas.

To find this person, you've typically incorporated various search tools such as your in-house database or Applicant Tracking System, the internet, social media, and other research tools and compiled an initial list of 15-20 folks to start calling. Upon reaching out by phone, your bottom-line goal is to generate interest in the assignment and encourage them to suggest other qualified folks to call. Sounds basic and doable. Doable -- yes. Basic -- hardly.

When I started in the business, I often identified people to recruit from target companies. Depending upon the size and scope of their present area of responsibility, I'd find those with a title such as the title of the position I was recruiting for. Several times I got lucky and found solid Candidates by this method. Yet, over time, I could have cast a wider net. Thus, I set about to stretch myself and find the most direct route to locating and recruiting even better-qualified Candidates. This was accomplished by building and nurturing a broad base of successful executives by periodically inquiring about their job satisfaction, career goals, and family life by demonstrating genuine curiosity and sincerest interest. The dialog was always win-win. This led to the reverse, where they were comfortable referring Prospects and other Sources to me.

As mentioned later in this book, note that I rarely approach anyone directly about a position. I'll typically present an enticing confidential executive search opportunity and ask if they know anyone who would benefit from hearing more about it in detail. Not that I wasn't proactive in encouraging one's candidacy when I knew in my gut that a match was on target. It's just that my nurturing approach often transitioned into recruitment conversations.

A proven and effective method to build and nurture a base of executives willing to provide you with solid referrals has always stayed the same. Your best results will come from establishing a tone upfront that engages the other person on the line in a compelling initial conversation, Incentivizing them to want to know more.

Present an enthusiastic, convincing, and thought-provoking concept about a search you are working on/managing within their industry or area of expertise. You respect their experience and would like to share some details confidently. You will often know of their interest within the first 15 to 30 seconds, depending upon their level of patience. Both parties must agree to continue the call or talk on another day and time. Or, they may tell me they have no time or interest and hang up.

If you are not credible, informative, and assertive up front, you've likely lost your chance to get this individual to invest more time to hear you out. I've always considered it prudent to make at least three solid attempts to call every name listed from any research conducted before walking away. Below are the four most likely outcomes from your outreach.

- The Contact expresses interest in the position and agrees to talk further.
- The Contact refers me to someone as a potential Source or Prospect on the current search.
- The Contact invests a few minutes sharing their background and accomplishments,
- so I may discreetly reach out if a fitting opportunity materializes.
- The Contact does not answer or return calls (after three attempts).

Regardless of how you've identified them, you'll want to extract something positive from the call whenever you speak with someone for the first time. After all, you've invested time to find this person, so take a few minutes to learn about their background and obtain any additional contact information. Always follow through.

If they express a lack of interest in continuing the call, ask if you may reach out in the future and discuss a search in which they may have a personal interest. Of course, you'll need to get their current title, their last few job titles, and where they currently fit within their organization. Failing that gesture, politely wish them a good day and end the dialog professionally.

If they never give you a chance, that's perfectly okay. That individual likely would not have been a great Candidate, and we would have had little control or influence over the outcome of their candidacy. But if you know their title, add them to your database and org charts. And those that have expressed interest or provided us with referrals or companies to recruit from should all go in our database, flagged, and tagged in such a way that we could reach them in the future for sourcing purposes or presenting a search assignment they implied would be a good fit for them.

Remember that you would know what a good match would be because you had taken the time to emphasize your sincere interest in them and understand what they would like to see in their next job. What don't they have now that they wish they had? What are their career goals? What position or scope of responsibility would be meaningful enough for them to look at and learn more about in the future?

> *Coming across as sincerely interested in someone's current role and future goals makes for the start of an ongoing, mutually beneficial relationship. More than 70% of the Prospects I've spoken to in this regard were willing to take calls from me, especially if they were to learn of unpublicized job opportunities that match their career goals.*

Wouldn't you appreciate a discreet recruiter who called you periodically, remained vigilant on your behalf, and presented opportunities in which you've expressed interest?

Furthermore, I would welcome the occasional phone call to help that recruiter with referrals of people I've worked with who are qualified or have expressed interest. I would also network the recruiter toward specific companies from which to recruit. An important thing to remember is to make every conversation a win-win and consistently strive to establish as many reciprocal relationships as possible. Personal and business ethics, genuine sincerity, and giving back to those we communicate with will pay dividends. We'll go into that more in-depth later.

I loved the business while in it, and I still do. I've relished completing an assignment and following up with the client and Candidate. The Candidate often cannot stop expressing gratitude for my first phone call to them about the position. And their family is happy and doing well (especially if relocation was involved). This satisfaction after an assignment, this elation of doing good in the world and helping an individual and family gain access to additional opportunities other-wise unavailable, is enormous. I've played an essential role by providing a path for many Candidates to progress in their chosen careers, increase their household income, and provide their family more lifestyle opportunities.

My desire for this guidebook is to assist the recruiter before, during, and after successfully making initial contact with a potential recruit. Regardless of how the next Source or Prospect you plan to reach was identified, your success on each initial call comes down to the following:

• Your ability to speak sincerely and enthusiastically about a client and the executive search you are working on/managing within their industry and area of expertise.

• Your confidential presentation of the opportunity succinctly with necessary details (never revealing Sources, if requested on any initial call).

By the end of that first call, your goal would have been to have classi-fied this person as one of the following:

- A **Prospect** who will ultimately evolve into a legitimate candidate for the current search.
- A **Contact** who will evolve into a legitimate referral **Source** for others they believe would benefit from hearing more about this position in detail.
- A **Source** who is knowledgeable about and credible within their industry, willing to describe their next career step or goal, and remains receptive when you eventually contact them to share such a position you are working on confidently.
- An individual who has no interest in talking, referring, or communicating with you at any time.

Get ready to explore a proven Search Methodology that has consistently delivered successful results throughout my career. We will dive into the most effective and strategic approaches for managing each step, tailored to the extent of your scope of responsibility. To begin, consider the following questions for yourself and your team:

- Is your role primarily focused on sourcing potential Candidates?
- Do you go beyond sourcing and initiate initial contact through phone or video platforms like Zoom?
- Are you responsible for conducting interviews, either immediately or at a later stage?
- Are you the designated recruiter accountable for presenting the Candidates to the client?

By addressing these key points, we will uncover the best strategies to streamline your search process and maximize your chances of securing exceptional Candidates.

Candidate classifications

Before we proceed, let me clarify the use of *capitalized* terms throughout this book. I am purposefully capitalizing **Contact**(s), **Source**(s), **Prospect**(s), and **Candidate**(s) throughout, primarily for clarification when referring to a human being.

Everyone I plan to contact for a specific search but have yet to speak to is considered a **Contact**. If a Contact has heard my elevator pitch but showed no interest in considering it, I reclassify them as an "**X-Contact**" for this search. Contacts who are dismissive or have no desire to listen are unlikely to change their stance in the future, at least for this search assignment. By doing this, we will know whom to avoid in the future.

As I begin to identify and speak to additional Contacts, it's only once I've talked to someone that I will know how to categorize/rank/flag them.

For example, a Contact becomes a Source by referring an individual for my search, either by providing the name of someone they know or suggesting a company or other entity from which to recruit would have their classification or designation changed (aka upgraded) to that of a **Source** for future sourcing purposes. It is essential to connect a Source to each specific search assignment for which they have referred someone.

The most common way to connect with the best Candidate for a job is through a Source. Therefore, it's essential to cultivate your relationships with Sources, keep track of their career paths, and periodically reach out to them with relevant information about job searches that align with their interests. I cannot stress this enough. It is also essential to express your gratitude for any recent referrals they have provided and let them know you may reach out to them in the future when needed.

When referring to someone as a **Prospect,** we would have already spoken, and I would have enough background information that it would make sense to get more in-depth about their career and the job we are discussing, initially through a second, more detailed phone call, and possibly a face-to-face interview with the recruiter before meeting the client.

I'll always keep them on my Prospect list until we've decided to meet with me face-to-face which, at this point, I would reclassify them as a **Candidate**. If, after the meeting, they fail to pass muster, I will re-classify them as mentioned in the next paragraph.

Even if I believe in advance that this individual is qualified and interested in the assignment, they will remain a Prospect until I've spoken more in-depth and decided to meet them in person. As you go through various stages of developing your Prospects, you may wish to add additional letters to denote them, such as ranking them in order of qualifications (Prospect-A, Prospect-B, Prospect-C), while someone no longer a viable Prospect for this assignment (Prospect-X). For those interested but not on target, keep their background information, label them a Source, and reach out to them for future searches.

Suppose they are qualified but uninterested and have yet to end the call. In that case, I'll inquire about their career goals, how I may help in that regard, and whom they know would benefit from hearing more about the position I referenced in this conversation. Don't immediately be dismissive; it is essential to remember that this person may be a terrific Source or even a Candidate for an alternate position down the road.

When I use the term **Research**, I refer to the efforts of recruiters who perform the hands-on work to identify and, at times, initially contact potential Prospects and Sources. For example, you may utilize an in-house research team or a custom software program everyone can access, hire an independent outside sourcing recruiter, or use an online ASP, digging through related industry organizations, industry membership directories, trade show attendee lists, and business cards from shows you've attended in the past, while researching newspaper and magazine articles, to name a few. Managing all these resources to move in sync from beginning to end is extremely important.

Retained vs. Contingency search

Information on the difference between Retained and Contingency search firms and all the other means companies employ to recruit and hire new employees is readily available online. But let me briefly share the basics and a couple of thoughts on my perspective.

Retained search firms are used to fill highly specialized, revenue-impacting, and (often) confidential leadership roles.

- Companies work in close partnership with one retained search firm exclusively for the duration of the search or an agreed-upon exclusivity period.
- Retained recruiters perform an in-depth vetting of Candidate qualifications.

- C-Suite level

Contingency search firms are used to fill the niche, individual contributor roles up to mid-level management positions (Director or VP level).

- Companies work in partnership with multiple contingency search firms to cover more ground.
- Employer performs an in-depth assessment of Candidate qualifications.

Search firms tend to recruit in a specialized area, such as accounting or law. Larger global search firms tend to be generalists or break up their search practice into different verticals managed by their separate business units.

As outlined above, relationships between contingency search firms and their clients are typically less intimate than in a retained executive search assignment relationship. Multiple contingency firms can sometimes be looking for the same recruit simultaneously. However, only the firm identifying the person who ultimately gets hired will get paid; everyone else walks away empty-handed.

Contingency search firms typically recruit for positions below $75,000 to $100,000 and are paid after the assignment and the new hire starts their new job. Retained firms recruit for positions that pay above those figures. Retained firms are paid their fee based on a percentage of the Candidate's final compensation, typically 25% to 33.3%. This is the ideal search firm/client-company relationship.

Since retained firms are paid over a three- or four-month period, with the first of three or four payments due at the start of the search, the client receives monthly invoices that contain business expenses created the prior month in connection with the assignment (i.e., cell phone allowance, travel expenses, and Candidate expenses).

With that personal stake, clients tend to be more present and involved early in the search process. Naturally, a more intimate relationship requires frequent contact with the client, which can grow into a long-term business relationship if managed appropriately.

Since most of my career was spent on the retained side, and due to the broader set of tasks and responsibilities required of the retained search firm, I am defaulting to refer to all search examples as retained executive searches.

Blending existing search firm processes with those in this book

Unless you're starting your own business, most recruiting firms have their methods and processes in place for searching. Management will decide who will place those initial calls and participate in the remainder of the search assignment through closure. I'll lay out methods that served me well as my searches moved from initial client Contacts to research and sourcing, meeting, interviewing, and presenting Candidates to clients, and through to getting an offer accepted and the Candidate showing up on day one.

The abundance of online research and sourcing options can make the process overwhelming. To ensure success, the client and recruiter must establish a mutually agreed upon and focused strategy. Additionally, all search team members should remain committed to their respective roles.

Before we move on, a quick word of caution: Prioritize your efforts by following your company's research best practices, sourcing policies, and standard operating procedures. When making these decisions, it is essential to consider company politics, budgets, staffing, and other relevant factors. Since process enhancement using my tools will be beneficial in the future, do your best to incorporate as much of this methodology as possible while concurrently adhering to established protocols and guidelines.

A Brief History of Sourcing and Recruiting

Thorndike Deland is acknowledged as an early pioneer in the recruitment industry, having established the first executive search firm in 1926. However, the profession truly began to transform in the mid-1940s. When I entered the search profession in 1980, the landscape had already started to shift. At that time, most small to mid-sized recruiting firms, including mine, did not use computers or have access to many tools, databases, online articles, job boards, LinkedIn, and other resources available today. Advancements in technology have accelerated the next generational changes in the recruitment function, revolutionizing how we operate.

Here are some interesting statistics about the executive search industry:

1. The global executive search services industry generated annual revenue of about $30 billion in 2021, according to Statista. According to a report by Research and Markets, the industry is expected to grow at a CAGR of 6.4% from 2021 to 2028.
2. The United States is the largest market for executive search services, followed by
3. Europe and Asia-Pacific.
4. The average fee charged by executive search firms for a single placement is around 33% of the Candidate's first-year compensation, according to the Association of Executive Search and Leadership Consultants (AESC).
5. The most common reasons for using executive search services are to fill senior
6. management positions, access a broader Candidate pool, and find specialized talent.
7. The technology industry is the largest market for executive search services, followed by finance and healthcare.
8. According to AESC, the average time to fill a senior-level executive position is around 3-6 months.

9. In the past 20-plus years, there has been a noticeable shift towards embracing diversity and fostering inclusion in executive search. This has led numerous firms to adopt policies and practices to promote diversity within Candidate pools and ensure more inclusive hiring processes. That said, with the recent Supreme Court rulings, that pursuit may be hampered.

10. According to a survey by Hunt Scanlon Media, executive search firms face top challenges, including competition from in-house recruitment teams, identifying and attracting top talent, and keeping up with technological advancements.

The Elevator Pitch, Research Tools, and AI

Early on, most recruiters had access to printed resources, such as published industry org charts, industry associations' printed membership directories, industry gatherings' attendee lists, business cards, internal organizational charts, etc. There were also online job boards and print ads. They brought in Prospects but were often not the ideal Candidate if hired because research and sourcing efforts were not used.

Not having early access to the internet or a computer to build a database may have seemed outdated, but it was a hidden advantage. It compelled me to plan. I learned to avoid unthinkingly reaching out to people based on lists from previous searches, directories, news articles, or recommendations from coworkers. Instead, I invested hours developing and rehearsing *concise, captivating* elevator pitches for initial Contact calls. Today, one has an advantage in utilizing AI tools to create the pitch.

In recruiting, an **"elevator pitch"** is a concise and persuasive introduction that a recruiter delivers to a prospective Candidate. It is a way to quickly and effectively communicate the critical aspects of a job opportunity, the company, and why the Candidate should consider it. The goal is to capture the Candidate's interest and make them want to learn more about the position and the organization. Like an elevator ride with limited time, an elevator pitch in recruiting is designed to create a compelling impression quickly. I've summarized my best elevator pitch execution tips below.

Integrate relevant research: Incorporating background research about the Contact into the pitch allows you to assess if the job title, responsibilities, and potential addition of P&L responsibility would benefit the individual.

- This information can be obtained from the referring Source or publicly available resources during initial research.

Reach out confidentially, without assuming personal interest: Your intention is solely to establish them as a Source, seeking their assistance in identifying and referring individuals who could benefit from hearing about the opportunity.

- Be brief, discreet, and gracious.

Follow-up and follow-through: Offer your time to discreetly provide more information about the position later and schedule your following conversation.

- During this future conversation, determine if a similar opportunity is already in progress at their current employer.

Initially, the **Applicant Tracking System (ATS)** was primarily used as a digital database to store and manage Candidate information. Over time, it has become a sophisticated tool streamlining the entire recruitment process. Modern ATS solutions now incorporate automation, AI-powered algorithms, and integrations with various platforms to enhance efficiency and effectiveness. These systems enable recruiters to seamlessly manage job postings, screen and track applicants, schedule interviews, and collaborate with hiring teams.

With the evolution of ATS, recruiters can use technology to optimize their workflows, improve Candidate experiences, and make data-driven decisions throughout the recruitment journey.

More recently, recruiters can leverage **Artificial Intelligence** in several ways to identify and attract top talent. Here are a few ways how AI can transform your work:

- **Automating Manual Tasks**: AI can help automate routine tasks such as resume screening. AI algorithms can analyze thousands of resumes and applications in an abbreviated time, focusing on keywords, skills, experiences, and other parameters set by the recruiters. This speeds up the initial screening process and allows recruiters to focus on the most promising Candidates. Note that while we are not anticipating, this effort will yield finalist-quality Candidates, although it can, it is more likely that they may be great resources of referrals.
- **Predictive Analysis**: AI can use predictive analysis to dictate the probability that a Candidate will possess the skills that match those required for a specific role. By analyzing data about a Candidate's skills, experience, education, and other attributes, and comparing these to the profiles of successful employees in similar roles, AI can provide recruiters with an estimate of a Candidate's likely success in a given position.
- **Sourcing Candidates**: AI can analyze vast amounts of data from various sources, like professional networking sites (LinkedIn), social media platforms, job boards, and company databases, to identify potential Candidates who may not actively seek a new position. These passive Candidates can often be an untapped source of talent.
- **Chatbots**: AI-driven chatbots can engage with Candidates, answer their queries about the job and the company, and gather initial information. They can even conduct preliminary interviews and rank Candidates based on their responses.

- **Enhanced Diversity**: AI algorithms can be trained to avoid biases, helping recruiters source diverse Candidates. They can ensure the process is fair and consistent, basing decisions solely on Candidates' qualifications and potential.
- **Candidate Engagement and Retention**: AI can help improve the Candidate experience by ensuring prompt and relevant communication throughout the hiring process. It can also predict which Candidates are most likely to accept an offer, helping to reduce instances of rejected offers.
- **Competitor Analysis**: AI can help understand competitor companies' hiring patterns and strategies, assisting recruiters to stay competitive and attract top talent.
- **Skill Gap Analysis**: AI can help identify the skills lacking in the current talent pool, which is useful when recruiting for future needs.

While AI can significantly streamline the recruitment process, it's essential to remember that it is a tool that aids human recruiters. AI can only partially replace the human element in recruiting: interpersonal connections, culture fit assessment, negotiation, etc. Therefore, the most effective recruitment strategy often involves AI-driven data analysis *and* human judgment.

No matter when you read this, whether in 1926, 1980 (when I started recruiting), or the present day, the one consistent tool throughout that timeline is the initial verbal contact. Any printed advertisement or position description can only do so much. Therefore, the recruiter's first communication must be compelling enough to encourage a follow-up call. Furthermore, your Sources and Prospects must recognize you for your consistency, dependability, confidentiality, and expertise throughout the process.

1

SEARCH METHODOLOGY

A: THE CLIENT ACCEPTANCE PHASE

W hile every phase of the retained executive search process could not exist without the other, this book focuses on what I consider to be the most decisive part of the search process: the identification, recruitment, and ultimate presentation of exceptional Candidates to your client.

In this first phase, I'll guide you through a long-established Search Methodology as you work on a new assignment and focus on gaining agreement with the client on all facets of the search. While meeting the client's Must-Haves for any position is crucial, the exact title and function of a search are *not fundamental for our purposes.* The processes I share apply to any job within our client's company. For example: discussing a specific skill set for a CFO versus an engineering VP or sales executive will not be necessary to understand and follow these recruiting steps and concepts.

For this volume, we'll begin with the understanding that your recruiting firm has secured the business. Upon the start of your assignment, you should already have a signed agreement letter and the first of several invoiced payments, often based upon 25% to one-third of the new hire's first year's annualized guaranteed income. Regardless of when the first payment and agreement letter between the recruiter and client have been signed, sealed, and delivered, there should be a face-to-face meeting before an official kickoff to any search, especially when the client/recruiter relationship is new or in its preliminary stages.

To gather the necessary information for starting a search, we have organized a collaborative meeting between key members of the client's team and your recruiting team. This session, held in a comfortable conference room setting, will span two to three hours, comprehensively covering every aspect of the search process. This thorough preparation is valuable and should be mandatory for all assignments.

Once the meeting is underway and initial introductions have taken place, it is essential for each participant to clearly outline their role in the assignment and their intended contribution to the search process. This ensures that everyone clearly understands their responsibilities and establishes a foundation for effective collaboration. Introducing and discussing the Search Methodology (see Appendix) that will guide our recruitment efforts is essential. This methodology will serve as a framework for our actions and provide a structured approach to conducting a successful search.

Our team and participating managers from the client organization will engage in comprehensive discussions to better understand their specific administrative requirements and expectations. We'll delve into the intricacies of their human resource needs, the underlying reasons for the search, the desired skill set they seek in the Candidates presented, and the client's process for onsite interviews. Alternatively, managers we have not yet met may question us about our firm and track record. Building an intimate knowledge of our client is paramount. It is crucial to remember that many of these details are sensitive and strictly confidential, never to be disclosed to anyone, especially the Candidates involved.

Clients often ask how long it will take to reach a successful conclusion in the search and get a new hire on board. I'll usually defer that answer to the end of the meeting after discussing everything. Before answering, I'll highlight my Search Methodology and recap and confirm the details just discussed in the forum, specifically how the client and my team agree to proceed. My searches, on average, took two to three months, some a bit longer. I've closed searches in less than a month, but I'll admit that any of those accomplished in under a month was due to the team working smart, a fluke, coincidence, pure luck, or any combination thereof. But once the client and I discovered common ground, I found them more flexible and forgiving, given our common goal. Still, ongoing scheduled communication between the recruiter and the client will increase the odds of a timely closure.

Supplementary Meetings

To establish credibility with your client, it is essential to proactively engage with the key executives involved in the search process via additional phone calls or meetings. You need to empathize with and understand the perspectives of the following stakeholders:

- The individual responsible for making the final hiring decision
- The influential opinion leader within the organization
- The dominant figure or "alpha" in the group
- The direct manager of the position being filled
- A senior-level individual considered a direct report to the position being filled

Observing the personalities and dynamics of managers in a group setting provides valuable insights into their unique characteristics, including the level of assertiveness exhibited by the dominant individual. It is also enlightening to hear diverse responses to questions regarding business plans, revenue targets, top priorities, and near-future plans. Even a 15-minute meeting can prove valuable to your search.

These intimate meetings are crucial in refining the qualities sought in Candidates, such as temperament, resilience, sense of humor, and overall presence. Understanding these key factors enables the identification of Candidates who align with the client's expectations and can positively contribute to their new organization.

By comparing the impressions of each manager following such meetings, one can gauge the level of consistency, teamwork, and trust within the team. This provides a brief insider's perspective on the company's culture, how it aligns with its reputation, and how potential sources or prospects may respond to being approached. Observing the personalities and interactions of the leadership team members sheds light on camaraderie, tension, and consistency of thought within the team. It also helps evaluate the cohesiveness of the management team and assess how they will collaborate with superiors, peers, and subordinates. (The experience may help you answer the following question for yourself as well: "Would I be proud and excited to present a well-qualified Candidate to this client?")

Whether working independently or collaborating with my search partners, I consistently prioritized establishing face-to-face or phone meetings with my clients. These individuals would directly supervise and interact with our chosen Candidate daily.

Understanding the organizational structure of each client was crucial in comprehending the hierarchy and the placement of profit and loss (P&L) responsibilities within the scope of the search. Depending on the size and breadth of the client, the division or business segment for which I was recruiting often had varying levels of interaction with other divisions. Whether it was a large corporation like Hughes, where we successfully recruited a division president for their communications division, or companies like Mattel or Citi, where we sourced executive leaders for specific divisions, effective communication with the client was necessary to determine the extent to which our Candidates would collaborate with other business units.

In the case of smaller clients without additional business units, the impact of the hired Candidates on the organization and its stakeholders is considerably more pronounced. This was evident in our recruitment efforts for companies like 3D Systems, CareCredit, and Petco. Whether placing CEOs, CFOs, engineering executives, or marketing leaders, given their track record, we were confident our selected Candidates would make an immediate and substantial contribution to the profitability and growth of these organizations.

A: THE CLIENT ACCEPTANCE PHASE

Okay, let's get at it. Here is where we begin our journey through the Search Methodology, with a meeting at our client's office as described above.

We must first define all aspects of our search assignment before beginning any Candidate research. Below you'll find a repository of questions to pose during client meetings.

I. Definition of Corporate Structure

First, we'll draw an organizational chart with the company's board of directors and senior officers at the top, following through with all the direct reports and their direct reports, as necessary. Next, we'll place the position we have been retained to recruit into the organizational chart and confirm to whom the position reports and what jobs report to this post. Next, several vital questions need to be answered:

- What is the company's structure and ownership? Is it a standalone privately held company, a public firm, or a larger organization's profit and loss (P&L) division?
- What is the financial situation of the company? Are they a start-up needing financing, or are they already profitable?
- What is the reporting structure within the organization, particularly from the position you are recruiting for, up the org chart to the firm's most senior executive?
- What are the specific products and services offered by the company and its division? Are the products manufactured in-house or outsourced to external entities?
- What are the required professional or technical skills, experience level, and educational qualifications for the position?
- Are there any significant business relationships, issues, objectives, or related plans within the company that should be considered?

- How does this company differentiate itself from competitors? What are its primary unique selling points or differentiators?

II. Definition of Organization & Assessment of Key Personalities

To ensure a successful fit for the position, it is crucial to understand the personalities involved and assess compatibility from the start. Gain an insider's impression of how the company perceives its culture, reputation, and public image from each executive's perspective. Take note of the overall atmosphere. Are they studious and serious, or is there a friendly and welcoming vibe? Pay attention to any competitive dynamics among the line managers and look for unique aspects that can help gauge whether your Candidate will fit into the team.

As you interview Prospects, you will probe for the personality characteristics the client would like to see and measure them against the traits you've personally observed with your client.

III. Definition of Job Assignment

Specifically, what are this Candidate's responsibilities and goals? How urgent is this search, and what is the reason behind the urgency? Is there a preferred closing date for this position, and what factors are driving that preference?

- **Required Technical Skills:** What are this role's primary responsibilities and critical focus areas? What specific skills are necessary for success in this role? Are there any preferred certifications or qualifications that Candidates should possess? What is the organizational authority: Does the Candidate have the authority to make hiring and firing decisions? Is there any P&L responsibility with this position?
- **Critical Problems and Timeframe:** What pressing problems or challenges must be addressed in this role? Is there a specific timeframe within which these problems must be solved?

- **Position Description and Growth Path**: How should this position's organizational responsibilities and authority be defined? What performance goals or objectives will the Candidate be expected to achieve? Is there a clear growth path or career progression associated with this role?
- **Desired Personality Characteristics:** What personality traits or characteristics would the client like to see in the ideal Candidate? Are there any specific cultural fit requirements or team dynamics to consider?
- **Incumbent and Transition Support:** Is someone in the role currently, and why are they leaving? Will the incumbent stay to support the induction of the new Candidate?
- **Elevating Candidacy and Relevant Industry Experience:** What specific skills, successes, or experiences would boost an individual's candidacy? Is there any preference for Candidates with vertical industry experience?
- **Growth Goals and Impact on Metrics:** Is the company focused on incremental growth, and what are the growth targets? Are profits trending upward, and how does this position contribute to that trend? How many new product or service launches are planned, and can the Candidate contribute? Will this position help lower the cost of doing business, and what metrics will be affected?
- **Performance Expectations and Timeline:** What are the candidates' goals in the first month, first quarter, or end of their first year? Are there specific milestones or deliverables expected within certain timeframes?

IV. Definition of Candidate

- **Cultural Fit and Interface:** Will the Candidate's personality blend well within their assigned part of the organization? How will they work with other business units they will regularly interact with? Are strong communication skills and charisma necessary for this role? Will the executive have ongoing interactions with customers?

- **Relationship Dynamics:** How does the Candidate fit and communicate with their immediate superiors, peers, and subordinates? Can they establish effective working relationships at different levels of the organization?
- **Strengths and Weaknesses:** What does the Candidate consider their primary strengths and weaknesses? How do these attributes align with the role's requirements and the organization's goals?
- **Must-Have Skills and Desired Qualities:** Identify the minimum skills needed for the role from the client's perspective, and rank-order them by importance. What other skills and attributes does the client desire in an ideal Candidate? Are any unique characteristics sought, such as turnaround experience or specific industry relationships?

V. Delineation of Critical (Must Have) Job & Candidate Characteristics Priority List

What skills does the Prospect or Candidate possess that match the Must Haves as requested by your client?

Does the client have any business policies or preferences requiring all management at this level to have earned a college degree and technical certification(s)?

The results of this question will act as a blueprint for our position description going forward. With the client's help, we will define the minimum skillset and experience the Candidates must have to excel at their job.

VI. Definition of Optimum (Have Done) Professional Background: College to Present

What significant contributions does this individual bring to the business? Have they already produced similar results for their current or past employers?

Review the Candidate's career history regardless of length during the bulk of their career. Focus on the years that show consistency, loyalty, upward mobility, revenue generation/contribution, and other accomplishments.

Has the individual jumped from company to company? Were these job changes logical, or were reasons for departure all over the map? Will the Prospect provide references to validate their explanation(s)? Have they met various goals requested by the employer?

VII. Definition of Compensation Package

When engaging in the recruiting process, it is essential to address the topic of total compensation early and often -- to ensure alignment between Candidate expectations and the client's offerings.

- **Flexibility of the client:** How flexible is the client regarding the total compensation package? Are there specific elements within the package that can be negotiated or customized?
- **Base Compensation Range:** What is the anticipated range for the base compensation? Determine the minimum and maximum figures for the position.
- **Bonus Structure:** Are cash bonuses guaranteed or performance-based? If performance-based, what metrics are used to determine bonus payouts?
- **Additional Benefits:** Inquire about the availability of stock options, health plans, retirement benefits, and other perks. Determine when these benefits come into effect, such as after a probationary period or upon employment.

VIII. Definition of Target Corporations

By compiling a list of similar and tangential companies and addressing the following questions, recruiters ensure compatibility, confidentiality, and successful search processes.

- **Cultural Fit:** Will the Candidate's current employer's culture blend smoothly with your client's? Is there potential for conflict or misalignment, primarily when referring to direct competitors?
- **Preferred and Excluded Companies:** Which companies are preferred sources for Candidates? Are there companies to refrain from recruiting from, and why?
- **Internal Candidates:** Has your client considered internal Candidates? How should you handle the relationship and recruitment activities, such as interviews and reference checks?
- **Sensitivity to Referrals:** Are there sensitivities or agreements regarding referrals from specific firms? If so, it will be crucial to exercise discretion with such firms.
- **Confidentiality:** Is the search assignment confidential within the company? When can the client's name be revealed?

IX. Acceptance of Assignment

As stated, the search agreement letter had previously been signed and agreed to. Therefore, at the end of the meeting at our client's office, with everyone's attention squarely on you, emphasize appreciation for their business, express excitement about your firm's part in helping grow this client's business, state that you look forward to working closely with everyone, and reconfirm your confidence in, and commitment to completing the assignment with the best available Candidate.

If you have yet to speak with any manager one-to-one, bring that up now. Then state that your firm is ready to execute the search as planned unless you've started with some early industry research and will maintain communication periodically, as discussed earlier.

Reinforce to the entire group that ongoing dialogue between recruiter and client is paramount to an efficient and successful search.

X. Confirming Letter to Client

Once your initial client meeting is over, you should write a summary letter containing the major bullet points and takeaways from your meeting and get it out to the individual who signed your agreement letter.

Start by stating that this summary description will be the basis for your search effort. Confirm its receipt and follow up to obtain the client's verbal agreement with its contents.

To avoid any embarrassment and issues, if not addressed at the meeting, it is necessary to know whom the client may have approached on their own before retaining your firm and how to handle any referrals that mention that individual. Follow up with written documentation in a confirmation letter to the client. I've had some clients mention they wanted a discount if their Candidate was hired. We agreed to take one of two avenues. Before starting a full-blown search, we would perform reference checks on this person for a lesser fee. Otherwise, we would communicate with this referral, present them in tandem with other candidates, and charge them our full fee. This must be addressed upfront, although I've discovered that clients' referrals rarely become finalists.

At this point, there should be no surprises here as enough validation and debate have already transpired.

XI. Documentation of Complete Specification

Let's not confuse the following with any documentation forwarded to our client.

On every search, I created a one or two-page document that I kept in a *sturdy file folder* at your desk and in digital form. This document contained two critical pieces of information: the search specification or position description, complete with every key data point about my client and the search assignment. Front and center was a second document, i.e., my 15-30 second summary script (or "elevator pitch").

Both files were accessible, opened, and in front of me whenever I discussed the assignment with Contacts, Sources, and Prospects. It became easier to remember with repetition after referring to it a few times while on recruiting calls, but it should still be kept nearby.

The one- to two-page position description contained important information on products/services, revenue size, the role I was searching for, its scope of responsibility across the organization, why the search is being performed, any unique upside potential, and what to avoid revealing at this point in the process.

When developing your elevator pitch, heretofore referred to as a "pitch," that is well-received, garners immediate intrigue, and creates an "emotional alliance" between a recruiter and Contact/Source/Prospect. It crafts a "gentleman's agreement" to delve deeper into the opportunity on this initial phone call or agree to a near-term date and time to talk further. ChatGPT and other AI programs can often assist in crafting your pitch.

In this pitch, we need to validate precisely what makes this job rare and offers an opportunity not available to this person at their present company or would elevate this person sooner rather than later. This is precisely why any advanced research into this Source/Prospect's background would be valuable in tailoring this elevator pitch to this specific person, thus making it more relatable.

Unless you already have some information about this Source/Prospect you would incorporate into your pitch, it should be generic. Create and practice speaking this 15-30 second elevator pitch. You won't have time to fumble and practice on the fly. The presentation must be brief and to the point yet enticing enough to leave the Source/Prospect wanting to know more.

Sit in front of your iPhone and video yourself promoting this position to an invisible Contact or place a family member or friend across from you. Practice this as often as necessary so you and your enthusiastic self are relaxed and uninhibited. Keep practicing until you sound confident and smooth yet professionally animated in your delivery.

Here are a few items to keep in mind when you give your elevator pitch to a Contact that you hope to elevate to Source or, preferably, a Prospect:

- Depending on the individual, is this position, scope, and title a significant enough advancement than may be available to them at their present company?
- Is there an opportunity for this individual to succeed with your client's state-of-the-art products or next-generation services versus their current employer?
- Would this role significantly elevate their industry stature and influence?
- Is there any upside potential for ownership or rapid advancement versus their current employer?

As stated, these are perfect examples of why it is worth taking the time to perform some due diligence before calling someone you have yet to speak with. Adding some personalization to your pitch can add impact and help increase their attention span.

Performing research on Contacts, Sources, and Prospects before calling them can benefit everyone by pointing out options they may have yet to consider when evaluating their career path.

I've had great success by investing the time to create and practice a pitch that generates interest enough to encourage this Contact to talk more in detail and turn this individual into a Source, if not a Prospect themselves. The worst that could happen is that they refrain from investing the time and hearing you out. However, if you can, at minimum, get your pitch heard to demonstrate the benefit to them personally, they're more likely to take time.

So now an organized set of criteria has been edited into an impactful, 15-30-second elevator pitch, concluding with the position's importance and the role's near-term upside. Emphasize what an "A+" Candidate could achieve and make it desirable. Again, any advanced research would help you personalize your pitch toward any specific individual.

Keep in mind your presentation is what I consider "the point of sale" or, if you're older like me, it's "where the rubber meets the road," a line from an old Firestone Tire commercial (YouTube.com/watch?v= 8HDGrrF92Qo).

XII. Review of Write-up with Client

If you haven't done so before, or if any substantial changes were made to the assignment by the client, make sure to follow up and review your previously sent position description to gain final agreement on your strategy for the search and that the summary writeup of the position description reflects the information agreed upon between you and your client company.

See the Appendix for an example of a position description summary we would send to clients for their agreement.

2

SEARCH METHODOLOGY

B. THE RESEARCH PHASE

I f your company's research function is already established, you might have handy a list with names, companies, job titles, and phone numbers of Contacts or Sources to call. But instead of getting stuck in the cycle of research, call, research, call again, and feeling like you need to make more progress, let's keep the momentum going during this research stage. We want to be diligent and proactive. So, let's start by focusing on the list of firms that you and your client agreed would be great places to find potential Candidates, both current and former employees. You'll lay a strong foundation for your recruitment efforts by thoroughly researching these and all other avenues for identifying Contacts to call. It will also enable you to provide valuable insights to clients, identify top talent, and develop effective strategies for successful placements.

Preferably, identify a minimum of 15-20 Contacts and Sources before you start reaching out. Having additional names to call helps maintain motivation and momentum, so devote time up front to build this list. Considering your current role, experience, and the caliber of your firm's research team should give you an idea of how long this process could take.

Let's agree that during the first several days, you will hold off calling anyone and focus on pure research instead. During this process, add any relevant data, such as salary, managers' and subordinates' names and titles, or any other relevant data, such as a recent press release or news story.

While gathering the data to build your list, stay alert for any additional current employee names within these target firms and add them to your organizational chart and search software platform. If you learn a former employee went to another firm, create an org chart for that new employer, even if it is the first person you have for that firm. Keep things current by noting any personnel changes or reorganizations you learn of. I've had great success connecting with former Sources and Prospects, regardless of when they left their firm, and sourcing them for peers from their past. Throughout my professional journey, I've consistently found that the most exceptional Prospects were referred to me by individuals with whom I have previously engaged or collaborated. Of course, this group of potential Candidates was receptive to my calls.

Depending upon any industry verticals and direct competitors my client was adamant we look into, I typically started with direct competitors after confirming there were no non-compete arrangements between them. Next, I probed related companies, depending upon the industry and Candidate skills required.

A company I mentioned earlier, 3D Systems, one of the very few in that emerging space during the early years of the 3D printing industry, needed a CEO. While there were relatively few direct competitors, we found the CEO out of a packaging company due to several similarities in their products' technology, manufacturing, and distribution.

After my firm placed the CEO of Petco, headquartered in southern California, still a tiny up-and-coming retailer, I was tasked with finding their next CFO. I recruited a VP & CFO from a Texas-based division of an overseas-headquartered furniture company. The successful Candidate was previously CFO of a 90-store home center firm, after which he was VP and CFO of his furniture firm, where he helped manage the start-up through an IPO. He was not appropriately rewarded at his organization and was willing to move his family to the West Coast for his significant equity deal. In this case, we found someone who, while relatively content, appreciated the adventure and the potential of the position and opportunity represented, which included an eventual IPO.

These two examples prove that we will sometimes identify qualified Candidates from direct competitors. Sometimes, you must be flexible and consider how seemingly disparate companies may have related processes and values. In both examples, we uncovered similarities in supply chain and experience growing a start-up retail business, even though the products were completely different.

B: THE RESEARCH PHASE

We will now discuss a reliable and established search methodology I have consistently leveraged with favorable results. We'll delve into the most efficient and strategic approaches for managing each step, irrespective of the extent of your specific responsibilities. Are you primarily engaged in sourcing? Or do you also undertake initial contact via phone? Will you conduct interviews through phone calls, video conferencing, and in-person meetings? Are you the recruiter entrusted with presenting Candidates to the client? We'll address these aspects comprehensively, providing a formal and precise understanding of handling each facet effectively.

I. Listing of Target Corporations

This process and its prep will be more impactful by calling Contacts with competitors from a list available from past related searches and any competitors suggested by your client. Understanding the business space and current dynamics will positively impact your production.

We'll begin with the initial list of target companies we created in collaboration with our client during the intake process. Our next step will be to broaden this list by including similar-sized-to-larger target firms or divisions of corporations. While it is permissible to add smaller firms, it's essential to do so only if we can identify a contact within them who possesses a relevant background worth pursuing.

It's worth noting that the chances of finding Candidates of the desired caliber within a company significantly smaller than our client are rare. However, let's not assume upfront that just because someone is with a smaller company, they will not possess the traits we seek. For example, our client has $650 million in revenue. However, one Contact you want to approach is currently the president of a small competitor that only generates $100 million. But we discovered that before this current role, he produced remarkable results for his two previous billion-dollar employers; his reason for joining the smaller firm as CEO was a potential IPO, which failed to materialize. Thus, we're sourcing this president for any referrals but making the pitch compelling enough to attract them.

Now, don't get me wrong. If I successfully engaged further with this president and realized the role was a perfect fit, I would encourage them to take an intimate, closer look before rejecting the opportunity outright.

We also want to consider companies on the periphery of the vertical market in which our client is doing business, as there may be companies in a related industry that might be a good fit. For example, if the job is sales or marketing-related, companies with sales to the same or a similar customer base may make them excellent targets. Should your client design electronic components and use the same overseas contract manufacturing entities, identifying Sources and Contacts in engineering or manufacturing roles in a related component vertical might be successful, too.

So, beyond your client's preferred target firms - which will be researched at the start of your efforts - we will build an expanded list of additional target companies, rank-ordered depending upon relevance in the same or related industry, the scope of an individual's responsibility, and revenue.

Competitive benchmarking and analysis should be doable depending on your firm's resources.

II. Listing of Related National Associations and Key Individuals

Our next step in broadening our outreach is identifying Contacts, Sources, and Prospects by researching national associations or other organizations related to our client's market. Companies may also belong to multiple membership organizations. Those membership lists are often public and available through an online association membership. Your focus should be twofold: targeting paid members, such as individuals from companies in that space, and targeting executives of the association itself.

Over the years, I have attended numerous industry conventions where I had the opportunity to meet and connect with various individuals. Some of them turned out to be excellent sources of information, while others became Prospects and Candidates for roles I was recruiting for. In a few cases, these interactions even led to establishing client relationships.

During these conventions, I always collected business cards from the booths and followed up with them either at the event or soon after, intending to source them (at first). Additionally, if I knew that a convention was coming up that made sense to attend, I would perform research beginning with a convention brochure, attendee list, or directory, printed or online. Next, I would connect with any appropriate Contacts that, by title, made sense to call. If I could connect with someone who appeared to be a promising Prospect and had mutual interest, I would arrange a meeting either at the convention hall or a different location. During these meetings, I would focus on understanding their career path and suitability for the assignment's Must-Haves while assessing their demeanor, attention span, enthusiasm, and alignment with my client. Over the years, these convention trips proved highly productive, particularly those involving face-to-face interviews. They justified the time and money invested, as they provided valuable industry insights and contributed to the overall success of the recruitment process.

At a minimum, reach everyone whose name you leveraged from Sources and follow up on those referrals. Whether or not they can help on the current search, consider investing a few minutes and getting to know their role and recent past, assuming they appear to be someone worth establishing a dialogue with. Get their brief current summary background into your database and flag them appropriately. Ask for consent to reach out periodically in the future about opportunities they've advised you would be of interest to them. The soft "ask" is a well-received best practice.

Stay current with their sentiment toward their current employer, whether their path to a more senior role is still viable, if their longer-term personal plans remained the same as when you last spoke, and whether their interest in a new position with a broader scope of responsibility remains.

Finally, assure them that their feedback will be held in the strictest of confidence. To keep your interaction fresh, do not hesitate to contact them strictly as a Source for other assignments you are conducting.

At this point, we've identified appropriately titled individuals from these organizational resources, called them up, and gained their interest and/or referrals.

III. Listing of Known Proven Sources in the Industry

This is where we take advantage of the effort we've invested in building out our database and flagging every individual you or your firm has connected with who was either a Source, Prospect, or Candidate for a past search.

Should you reach out to someone you've placed in the past, and you know they are still employed at the firm where you've placed them, make sure they are firmly aware you are calling them as a Source only. *This is important.* Add to that conversation that you are concurrently checking in to learn how things are going, and you would like an update about their current job and whether their expectations have been met. Is the family still committed to your placement's success?

You will eventually begin to see the benefit of returning to folks you have contacted in the past who were willing to take your calls, partly because we discussed our mutual desire to stay mindful of any position for them due to their solid understanding of their industry.

IV. Comparative/ Priority Rating of Target Corporations

Depending upon any requests from the client, we'll want to prioritize our target list, thus giving us a logical order of the call process.

We will want to start with those firms identified with your client followed by the other direct competitors, but in order of revenue for the entire business unless one or more business unit(s) exists under this individual's scope. Clients typically want Candidates with P&L ownership above your client's current revenue.

On the other hand, if a client is a $50 million company, although there may be qualified people in firms generating less than $50 million, we agreed with the client when they stated that they would prefer someone from a firm with over $100 million in revenue to bring that mentality and skill set over to our smaller client, thus helping them get to $100 million and beyond.

That said, we still need to invest time to find someone that came to a smaller revenue firm for equity or other unique reasons, so I want to take advantage of an opportunity to speak to them. We need to be sensitive that while specific Prospects may want to avoid taking a step back in revenue responsibility, the upside potential and benefits make sense to them to move to a smaller revenue company. Regardless, we will still focus on the $100 million and higher revenue companies at the beginning out of respect for the client.

Your best means of finding quality recruits is to search and locate Contacts and potential Sources just above, at, and immediately below the approximate revenue level of responsibility you are searching for.

At this point in our research, we are beginning to expand our understanding of a target company's organizational charts. By now, we should have already started a listing of this group of Contacts that we plan to call by adding their names and titles, as well as others discovered along the way, into our org chart program in real-time.

Focus your continuing research on determining the size and shape of any divisions, groups, or business units to determine where we need to recruit from within each company. For example, we may be recruiting for a vice president of manufacturing for our client who may not come from a target firm's corporate side but rather from a

THE EXECUTIVE RECRUITER'S PLAYBOOK | 53

specific division. Therefore, depending on how revenue is spread throughout the target business, there may be a senior vice president of manufacturing at a corporate location. Yet, there may be divisions of the appropriate size that may have their heads of manufacturing based at the unit's manufacturing facility and report to the corporate leader. Hence, before we start calling, we will initially look to understand each firm's structure, followed by targeting calls to the appropriately sized division or unit.

It is always preferable to perform advanced research on each company before calling. Utilize information from your database, LinkedIn, basic Google searches, LEXIS-NEXIS (if applicable), Google or Yahoo's finance sites, or any other resource to give you an understanding of the corporation size and business unit revenue within each firm you plan to call.

When you start making calls after identifying your initial 15-20 names, you'll continue performing additional research concurrent with making calls to new Contacts, maintaining your momentum. For example, by the end of most of my searches, I'd have spoken with anywhere from 50 to 200 individuals.

V. Development of Organizational Structures of Key Target Corporations

This step is straightforward. With all the available resources at your disposal, you should be able to piece together an organizational chart of your client's direct competitors, enough to help target one or more Contacts at the appropriate level from these firms and turn them into Sources, if not Prospects.

VI. Listing of Sources in the Key Target Corporations

Key target companies refer to the list of competitors or other target businesses you and your client agreed makes sense to recruit from. Once we have identified Contacts in a direct competitor, you may find one or more of those will become Sources or Prospects, depending upon the breadth and depth of prior database entries. But suppose your recruiting firm's business model is recruiting within a narrow vertical marketplace. In that case, I suspect you would likely have more than one Source or Prospect from a direct competitor identified from an earlier search.

Please ensure you reach out to individuals whose titles might appear overqualified for the position you are searching for; I have had Prospects with regal-sounding titles which became excellent Prospects or Candidates. Remember only to approach these individuals as Sources.

Industry periodicals, online articles, newspaper announcements of promotions (possibly a source back into their previous firm), industry organizational directories, trade shows, etc., are abundant resources.

VII. Listing of Corporate Officers Who Recently Left Target Corporations

Encourage anyone you've ever had an interest in maintaining a dialogue with to keep you current with their contact information, primarily for any future searches they may have interest in or, in this instance, to call them as a Source of names of recently departed individuals from their current employer. For those you are not referred to, there are newspaper articles, press releases, LinkedIn, Google searches, etc., to get an assist in finding individuals who left a firm you wish to network into and recruit from.

Once reached, after congratulating them about their new position, you'll want to create a win-win scenario with the call. Request they keep your name, number, and email in their phone's directory and share that you are interested in tracking their career and contacting them should you have a search that fits their career goals.

It rarely happens, but there have been publicized career changes that failed to work out. Imagine learning about the career change of a person within an industry that your firm recruits, reaching them to congratulate them, and encouraging them to retain your contact information, even if they have a great relationship with the recruiter that placed them at their new firm. It could be a few months later or a few years, but I have had a few individuals reach out to me as Prospects after our initial call. Their reasons for leaving, or considering leaving their latest employer, varied. Regardless of the reason, they were now requesting my help.

VIII. *Preparation of Priority Sources*

You have put together your initial list of 15-20 Contacts; preferably, it would include those identified from direct competitors. Added to this list, we will hope to find Sources, Prospects, or Candidates from past related searches, which we will refer to as "priority Sources" (as they are proven commodities having been "tested" via past conversations while conducting a related search).

Reach out to learn how they are doing, ask for referrals, and close with gaining their perspective and sense of the current industry landscape in which you are recruiting. Be gracious and clarify that you value insight from their vantage point.

IX. *Preparation of Preliminary Prospect List and Comparison to Job Write-up*

As we put together our list before we start calling, we will prioritize those labeled as Contact, Source, Prospect, and Candidate (the latter three from past searches) that compare most favorably to our job description and Must Haves.

As you gain traction and excel in this part of the Search Methodology, making calls concurrent with your research will be more beneficial and efficient.

But for now, gather your list and, to the best of your ability, compare your industry research and knowledge of these individuals against the bullet point requirements of the job summary created earlier with your client. Once you have done so, rank the list from one to X, perfect your pitch, and prepare to start calling.

X. Define Target Organizational Level for Each Corporation/ Define Corporate Compensation Policies

We often identify divisions or P&L centers when recruiting from large target companies. We will then attempt to identify all Contacts of a specific function within each business unit. We will make calling a strategic process by initially reaching out to those you believe your position level would be attractive. Save the others for later, if necessary. Also, *be careful about calling too many Contacts within the same firm for the same position*; word gets around, and it may come back to haunt you.

At a minimum, Candidates you will submit either need to at least have had enough experience at the lower revenue range of your search to be viable, or they interview so well that there was no concern about their ability to ramp up and show they can manage in a higher revenue business than presently.

You have already established that your client will provide real incentives, enough to encourage potential Prospects to take a closer look. As an extreme example, assume your search assignment is for the vice president of manufacturing for a widget company with revenues of $100 million. Yet, someone you have identified runs a $650 million widget manufacturing business unit within his current employer. So, what might incentivize that individual to look at our job? Could our job provide the near-term potential to become CEO of the corporation, own a percentage of the firm, or any other attractive option that might offer a significant upside?

Once you contact an individual, do your best to engage them and, at minimum, get a sense of revenue and compensation within their business unit for their role. For most public firms, only the senior employees' salaries are public. This information may also help identify the appropriate division within larger companies from which you are recruiting.

XI. Contact Sources per Priority Listing

NOTE: Do NOT begin calling anyone on your list until you have read the subsequent chapter entitled "Prospect Development Phase."

Regardless of when we begin calling Contacts and Sources, most, if not all, will be first-time calls.

I want you to first be creative, barnstorm with peers, and use ChatGPT or similar methods to develop and refine your elevator pitch and these outbound voicemail messages when attempting to reach your Contacts and Sources for the first time. Your firm may have trained you, you've fallen back into older calling tactics, or you're simply winging it with little preparation. But you realize your results could be better.

That said, before we move on, let me give you one approach for reaching executives you want to connect with for the first time, one that has worked for me 99% of the time. Whether I'm talking to a secretary, leaving a voice message, or sending an email, they all may appear on the surface to be "private," "secure," or "personal." Rest assured, more often than not, if your Contact is at a certain level, they'll have an associate or assistant that listens to or reads your communication, so you'll need to be consistent and discreet in your message(s).

Understand it's not my desire to create controversy for my book and ask any reader to compromise their standards and ethics when attempting to be aggressive and proactively reaching out to a Contact. But our job is to get through to them. Therefore, in feeling optimistic about my messaging that follows, I am factoring in the good I sincerely believe I am doing by reaching this Contact and advising them of an opportunity they will likely not otherwise hear about - until it's over. Given their current role, I anticipate they would appreciate learning of a position that will be a richly rewarding opportunity for the right person, possibly themselves or someone they know who would be a great match. I've used the following dialog thousands of times with tremendous success. My tone was always respectful and professional but firm.

State your name and firm and that you are calling to reach [EXECUTIVE'S NAME]. Their name was given to you by "another individual" as a "confidential professional (or personal) reference" on them.

If pressed for the reference's name, simply and confidently state you're not at liberty to share that information as the "individual" in question is gainfully employed and requested anonymity. You can only reveal that name upon speaking directly to [EXECUTIVE'S NAME].

If the person taking the message balks, which is rare, repeat the anonymity statement.

Failing that, politely urge the assistant to pass along your name and phone number and let [EXECUTIVE'S NAME] decide whether to call me. State the importance of this call and that you hope you both can agree to leave it up to [EXECUTIVE'S NAME] to follow up.

Worse case, you can call after hours and leave a similar message as above on the Contact's voicemail. If you maintain a similar posture by stating you are calling [EXECUTIVE'S NAME] to perform a reference, your odds of getting a call back significantly improve.

Once you connect with your Contact or Source and they begin by asking whom this mysterious person is that provided their name as a reference on them, state there was no reference in this instance; however, you have two goals.

One goal was to reach them discreetly to advise them of a confidential search. Your second goal was to phrase a message that removes anyone's suspicions that an executive search firm was attempting to recruit them.

Their current role (and industry credibility, if you have background information) led you to believe they understand the industry well and may know of someone who would benefit from hearing about the assignment. They will either express personal interest, refer someone, or pass on helping. If they pass, ask about their future plans and if you may reach out should a related search come to pass.

99.9% of those individuals I've reached in this manner were flattered by my proactive approach and making sure we connected. Only one person over the years told me my method was unethical and that I wasted their time. To them, I sincerely apologize, as that was not my intention.

For a minute or two before I start my sourcing calls, I internalize the validity of the search, the good I am doing by helping individuals advance their careers, and affirm that the majority of the best Candidates are "passive," meaning they are gainfully employed and not currently looking to change jobs. However, under the proper circumstances, they may be open-minded enough to listen further, whether for themselves or someone they have in mind to refer to you.

Unless you have information about an interested referral, remember that everyone we call the very first time will be flagged as a Contact when placed onto our list of people to reach. You may also have some Sources, Prospects, or Candidates from past comparable searches on that list. Only once we have connected on the phone would we re-label them as, for example, a Source or Prospect.

If a Contact I speak to refers someone to me who expressed interest in my search, I will label the referring party a "Source" for this specific search and the interested person a "Prospect," but only if they meet the Must Have requirements.

Unless I know of a referral's interest in the assignment, I will *always* approach everyone else as a Source. I've learned that acting too assumptive upfront about someone's interest level can be taken negatively, and we want to avoid that. Only once we have made contact will we know how to classify them. No rocket science here.

Regardless of how the individual you plan to call was identified, that initial Contact will usually be a phone call. Your ability to prepare properly before you make the call and build rapport, especially during your initial conversation with a referral, is pivotal to the success of your search assignment. Once you have presented a compelling and thought-provoking job opportunity with sincerity and enthusiasm, the other party will either continue the call (for themselves or to refer someone), agree on another day and time to talk, or politely end the dialogue. Depending upon their patience, you will often know their interest in talking further within the first 60 seconds of the call.

Once you begin making sourcing calls to everyone on the list, start calling those listed as Sources, then Contacts next and in the strategic order we placed them.

Depending on the quality of your research and the professional enthusiasm of your pitch, you should be able to expand the list to 40, 50, or even more than 100 within a couple of weeks, if not sooner. I have filled searches with fewer, but the searches were in narrow vertical markets.

When appropriate and time permitting, after qualifying (or disqualifying) the referral and seeking advice on whom to call that may be a good match or resource, take a reasonable amount of time to understand the background and career goals of the person on the call. People typically open up once you have established a legitimate rapport. For example, encourage them to share what they would like to see in a new job to consider making a change. Nothing heavy or too deep, as it is not an in-depth interview. Ask about their current position title, P & L, scope of responsibility, team size, location, and anything unique. Have this dialogue regardless of their lack of interest in leaving because it adds value to your rapport; that Contact knows of your genuine interest in them, which may evolve into a mutually beneficial relationship.

And - no surprise here - get them into your database. As your network of Sources increases, it should also increase in depth by filling in names and titles on your organizational chart program. Whether you experience beginner's luck or not, building out these org charts takes time. Unless you invest the time or money to add more research support, pay an outside researcher, join an organization that provides member lists freely, or attend industry events yearly, you will be digging for data.

As stated earlier, 95% of the people I have placed over the years have been referred to me by Sources. Many of those referred to me became additional Sources and Prospects; others became Candidates, a few were of no help, and some I needed help locating.

XII. Contact Prospects per Priority Listing

NOTE: Do NOT begin calling anyone on your list until you have read the subsequent section entitled "Prospect Development Phase."

When speaking with someone with whom your gut and research tell you should qualify as a Prospect, you will want to build rapport, letting them know that you recognize the value of their credentials and respect how they have presented themselves. You will invest time to gain further insight into their background and achievements for the current or future searches. Politely ask what kind of opportunity it will take for them to consider changing jobs seriously and when.

Imagine the future power of a rock-solid contact database meticulously built over multiple years, populated with individuals you have taken the time to get to know and enjoy a win-win relationship. Whether you are building your database or adding to an existing one, the Sources and Prospects, even Candidates you have personally met in person or over the phone, will only enhance and add credibility to your database. However, ensuring it will never become a one-way street i.

The manner in which you conduct yourself, especially during your initial call and, of course, all subsequent conversations, should yield multiple benefits. This person on the other end of the line may become a potential new Prospect if not a viable Source. But even more surprisingly, I have had several become future clients. Their reasoning for hiring me was primarily due to my *consistent* profession-alism and credibility when communicating with them. And the fact that I let them know that I would like to maintain an open line of communication in a mutually beneficial capacity played a significant role. They realized our relationship would not be one-sided, with me constantly asking for referrals. Instead, I would approach them occa-sionally with an opportunity they have implied would interest them.

With time and patience, you will learn that the tone of your voice can reveal a lot about you and disarm a guarded Contact. Do you sound confident and professional? Do you sound as if you have an exciting and legitimate reason for calling? Can you quickly summarize the purpose of your call and gain their interest?

Before starting my calls, I tested the elevator pitch on peers (and, at times, my wife) to gauge my ability to grab their attention. Better yet, assume up front that the Contact will not be able to spend more than a minute with you on the phone; therefore, you'll state your pitch and find a date, time, and number to call to go into more detail. I would rather have this individual in a place where they can listen, take notes, and ask questions. Remember to listen for cues on the other end of the phone. Is your Prospect speaking from their Bluetooth while driving? Do they seem distracted or skeptical? Be an expert observer and adjust accordingly. If the timing of your initial call is inconve-nient, discuss their next available time when you can go into detail, and they can speak candidly.

If my pitch had been effective, I would not have been concerned that the potential Source or Prospect would ghost me the next time we planned to speak. It has happened, but rarely. Sometimes, Contacts are enthusiastic upfront but change their mind overnight. But, of course, this only proves to me that they were not viable.

If my only alternative were to leave a message, I would leave my elevator pitch on the voicemail. I would then reach out up to two additional times to make contact.

Assuming I have reached them on the phone, after introducing myself, I would give the Contact my intriguing pitch about the position, *immediately* followed by a request to learn of anyone they believe might be interested in hearing more about this position in detail. By not asking upfront if they are personally interested, I am not taking the opportunity away from them, but - instead - addressing them as a knowledgeable industry source who may know someone qualified for the job.

And if my elevator pitch struck a nerve and this individual had an initial personal interest, you can be confident they will express that interest without you pressing the idea. And by not approaching a Contact or Source directly for the job often triggers subconscious thoughts that naturally get them evaluating the opportunity for themselves. Whether or not personal interest is eventually displayed, I am confident I have placed that thought in their mind for consideration at some point.

You are also not potentially putting them on the defensive; they may be at work, near their peers, and unable to speak candidly. Or perhaps they're in a mentally focused state that makes continuing the conversation difficult and awkward. At this point, you would ask, "if not now, when is the next opportunity to speak with you, and at what number can you be reached?" Then make sure you keep that commitment. The demeanor revealed in the Contact's reply provides insight into how to proceed with the conversation. Only as a last resort, email a brief job description without revealing the client's identity.

Expect to follow up to the bitter end with *everyone* whose name has come up in your research and sourcing calls. If you cannot reach someone, try again, perhaps even one additional time for three attempts maximum. Leave no stone unturned.

It is a two-step process for moving forward with viable Prospects.

Step 1: Initial calls must occur for you to generate enough interest on their part and let you collect enough background information to produce a summary resume addressing your client's Must-Haves. This also sets the stage for comparison to other Prospects.

Depending on your client's timeframe, how long it's taken you to finish the bulk of your research and make headway with Contacts, Sources, and, yes, their referrals, it is anticipated you will eventually gain serious interest on the part of at least three, four or five Prospects from which you will move forward and take next steps.

Step 2: A second, more detailed conversation must occur on the phone so we can gather even more background detail to be sure that you can discuss each viable Prospect with your client and gain consensus to meet the Prospects in person for further evaluation. These steps increase the odds that your face-to-face interviews will produce positive results consistent with your initial impressions.

Remember that having a second string of qualified prospects is always beneficial in case one of your preferred Prospects falls off. So, keep performing additional research in the background to the degree you have time.

If you have more than three qualified Prospects and you plan to meet the top three or four before any client interviews, always keep the second-string Prospects interested (i.e., "warm"). I've advised these Prospects that the client asked to meet three other Candidates at the start but may decide to see more. You'll keep them updated as soon as you learn of next steps. If they are confident in their capabilities, there should be no problem with them remaining patient, knowing you will follow up in due time as you have met all previous commitments with them.

As a constant reminder, always be on time, prepared, and focused in every communication with each Prospect, Source, and Candidate, as it will increase their desire to receive future calls from you or reach out to you for assistance.

Let me rephrase that because this is key. Every one of the businesspeople you source and network with - starting with your initial contact with a Source or Prospect - is pivotal to the success of your search assignment and closing of future searches. Setting and maintaining a high standard in the preparation and execution of all communication is tantamount to accomplishing your end goal: building rapport, acquiring information that leads to identifying ideal Candidates, closing the search and satisfying your client, getting paid, and building a robust referral database in the process.

There is an old phrase attributed to multiple individuals over the years, and it goes something like this: "There's never a second opportunity to make a first impression." Know this to be accurate, as you will rarely, if ever, get a second chance at making that crucial first impression.

XIII. Contact Associations for Additional Source Development

Depending upon the results of your initial research into nationwide industry associations and subsequent phone calls to identify key individual Sources and Prospects, you should concurrently research Contacts identified through regional industry organizations, committees, associations, and other groups' member rosters, online articles, LinkedIn, etc. We're not duplicating our previous efforts inside these entities but simply digging deeper to ensure we have thoroughly delved into as many resources as possible for potential Sources and Prospects.

As mentioned previously, I often attended several industry convention shows yearly. I spent a good day or two meeting with potential Sources and Prospects, depending upon the timing of my search and the industry event. These are excellent places to pick up the business cards of those you could not otherwise meet and truly understand the specific product or service vertical you are recruiting for. Identifying options for adding names to your database and org charts for future research should become a habit.

XIV. Prepare Individual Prospect Detailed Professional History and Source Comments

At this point, you have successfully identified and engaged with enough Contacts and Sources. You have a shortlist of Prospects who meet the Must Haves, have expressed their agreement to proceed, and demonstrated good communication skills and responsiveness.

Take the background information from your prior phone conversation(s) with your Prospects, double-check that you have identified as many Must Haves as possible, and create a summary resume (one-pager, ideally) without excessive detail. You can always go deeper into each background when speaking to your client.

Especially if your client relationship is still new, your client will most likely want to discuss the Prospects you believe are qualified and that you plan to interview face-to-face before presenting them to your client, thus incurring expenses and time. Recruiters in longer-term, successful client relationships usually do not need permission to meet with prospective Candidates, as you have justified this part of the methodology in the past with successful results.

Many search firms use video conferencing, Zoom, etc. But for most of my peers and me, nothing was more insightful and credible than a face-to-face encounter.

That said, by having ongoing phone calls or meetings, your client would know your progress and whom you have recruited. Periodic check-ins allow the client to provide real-time feedback on folks you are currently developing or plan to meet. This process helps us confirm that we are on the right track. We want to avoid investing time in someone the client would have rejected.

Once we have made significant strides and found several qualified Prospects, we will follow the steps in our next Chapter, the "Prospect

Development Phase," and gather more detailed background information via phone and (later) in person. Through these interviews, we will dig deeper into their interests, qualifications, and needs, including family concerns, compensation, and meeting availability.

Keep your notes updated and handy, as referring to them during client progress calls will be necessary.

XV. Comparisons of Prospect Data to Search Specification

After we have narrowed the group of Prospects (by interviewing over the phone), we will create a short list of quality leads. By comparing their qualifications with the Must Haves, accomplishments, scope of responsibility, and years of experience, we can decide who appears the most qualified and worth an in-person meeting.

XVI. Prepare Prospect Priority List

We will then rank the Prospects, discuss the list with your client, and confirm whom you plan to meet in person.

HARNESSING THE POWER OF ONE OF YOUR MOST ESSENTIAL QUALITIES

"Bet on people, not on strategies."

— *LAWRENCE BOSSIDY (RETIRED CEO OF ALLIEDSIGNAL)*

One thing all successful recruiters have in common is that they're target-driven. It's an essential quality to have in such a competitive industry where performance-based pay is a common feature. Your success hangs on your ability to identify and secure the best talent to meet a specific end goal: Your focus on that target is essential.

Perhaps it is this quality that makes the industry such a rich environment for continuous learning and self-improvement. You need to keep ahead of the changes, not just in the recruitment industry, but in all the fields you're serving. It's this drive that led you to this book, and it's this drive that feeds your determination to do everything you can to accelerate your skills and success rate. It's the same drive that inspired me to write this book in the first place.

I see an opportunity here, not only to help individual recruiters make it to the top of their game but also to amplify the success of the industry at large… and for that, I'll need your assistance.

In order for me to share these skills with as many recruiters as I can, thereby leveling up the whole industry, I need to make sure that everyone who's looking for this training finds it – and you can make it more visible by leaving your honest feedback.

By leaving a review of this book on Amazon, you'll show other recruiters where they can find the information they're looking for and, in turn, give the whole industry a boost.

Simply by letting other readers know how this book has helped you and what they'll find inside, you'll guide them toward the resource they're looking for.

Thank you for your support. When we level up together, the whole industry benefits.

3

SEARCH METHODOLOGY

C: THE PROSPECT DEVELOPMENT PHASE

Once we've reached someone who has expressed interest and appears qualified, we'll expand upon our previously collected data.

Since you've already connected with this individual and have some basic background information, we'll use this follow-up call to expand upon the summary resume developed from our initial call. We'll dig deeper into each Prospect's background at this time, which we must perform before committing to meeting in person. If your Prospect is genuinely interested, they will not express concern that you are calling again for even more background information.

Once we've taken a deeper dive into the Prospect's history and are confident this Prospect is on target with the assignment and meets your high standards, beginning with our next chapter, we'll start with in-person interviews between the Prospect(s) and you, the recruiter, as you consider each worthy of meeting the client.

C: THE PROSPECT DEVELOPMENT PHASE

I. Contact with Prospects per Priority List

Up until now, you've gathered enough data from each Prospect to share a summary resume with your client addressing, at minimum, the Must Haves and briefly the Prospect's job history, scope of responsibility, education and approximate compensation range, and any standout accomplishments that separate this individual from others.

As implied earlier, depending upon your relationship with your client, you may need their consent before you invest additional time on a lengthy phone call with Prospects whose candidacy you've decided to pursue. Once your client gives you the go-ahead, contact those selected Prospects over the phone if that coordination is necessary.

II. Brief Definition of Client, Assignment, and Position Responsibilities (*Client is not Identified*)

When placing these subsequent sets of calls to Prospects since gaining a thumb's up from your client to pursue them, it's often time to share more detail about your client, depending upon what and how much you've been permitted to share up until now. Some clients allow generic descriptions of their firm without confirming their company name, while others are okay if confidentiality is maintained. So, let's be sure to verify your options up front.

At the beginning of these conversations, I usually asked for verbal confirmation to maintain confidentiality about our client and this search assignment, even if the Prospect has a suspicion of who my client may be.

At the beginning of the call, I'll let each Prospect know that their career history and expertise align with the credentials I'm looking for in an individual for my client, and I would like to explore their background further in-depth. It is often at this point that I'd reveal the identity of my client, assuming I was authorized to do so.

When providing a summary overview of the client, align the role and responsibilities with your Prospect's ambitions and professional goals. Emphasize the areas they found attractive when you first discussed the role. Promote the uniqueness of the opportunity and how it benefits them.

As a side note, many clients don't want their identity disclosed until necessary because they want the minimum number of people to know this search is real. For example, if word gets out, their competitors, customers, business partners, and suppliers may forgo seeking the facts and assume the worst. In these instances, the client would prefer controlling the narrative.

III. Define Complete Details of the Professional History of the Prospect with Emphasis on Current Responsibilities, Achievements, and Problems

This next call to each Prospect will be our second interview call to discuss their background.

Make sure to cover as much ground as possible on these calls. At this point, we've got to be sure each Prospect we interview meets and exceeds the minimum skills and other characteristics described in the position description created and agreed upon between your client and you. We must also remain vigilant regarding any issues that creep in and blindside you, suddenly preventing a Prospect from pursuing the assignment.

Remember that this second, albeit more profound, conversation about each Prospect's background, beyond what was captured through your initial phone conversation, might appear redundant since we anticipate meeting face-to-face to gather yet more background data and with an emphasis on observing them face-to-face. The supplementary information retrieved during this additional call is necessary; besides more in-depth background information, it helps ensure that we move forward with Prospects whose facts and statements are consistent across all conversations, who are proactive and responsive in their communication with you, and who remain sincere about their candidacy.

With this in mind, let's go into more detail about the information we need to develop on this subsequent call to Prospects.

During these Prospect phone interviews, you will probe further about the Must Haves, wins, and losses, strengths, limitations, insights, unique attributes, their job-related technical skills, issues with fellow employees, any events requiring discipline, how the job we're discussing might affect their personal/family life, confirmation nothing has changed, and their interest remains strong. Understand what drove their career decisions to change employers and explore further about them, including hobbies or outside activities, job change or relocation issues, and anything that will impact the family due to a change in employers.

During these in-depth calls, subtly ask for titles reporting to them and to whom your Prospect reports. If names, titles, or anything noteworthy is mentioned, make a note and add them to your org chart program.

IV. Prepare Prospect History Summary

This Prospect History Summary should be in a resume format, not an original resume from the Prospect themself. Any resumes you send to your client should be on your letterhead and similarly formatted for all Prospects making a clean, professional, and consistent presentation. A few clients requested an original resume; we accommodated their request after the Prospect provided consent. We then sent the Prospect's original resume but placed it in its proper place, that of physically behind our version in the envelope. If emailed, place your firm's version first and above the Prospect's.

Your notes on each Prospect are to be considered works-in-progress, updated after each phone conversation. After your ultimate face-to-face interviews and you decide whom to present to your client, you'll find composing the three-to-five-page Candidate letter easier by referring to this ever-evolving set of notes (see the Appendix for two examples of Candidate letters).

V. Probe Details of Critical Factors of Assignment

In your detailed Prospect summary, you'll emphasize to whatever degree our Prospect aligns with the Must Haves and any other skill the client wants to be addressed. This should be a deep dive as we want the Prospect to provide examples or validate business decisions that parallel our client's needs.

Assuming your relationship with your client is one of trust and confidentiality, in part due to what we'll call "recruiter/client privilege," we should also be in a position to know anything unique about our client's current situation, be it a financial issue, an internal political problem, even an issue affecting your client's industry for which you will need to stay current regarding how that may affect the position for which you are recruiting. For example, the client may be experiencing a downturn in sales in one region; they just lost a large division's general manager to a competitor; their vice president over manufacturing just retired. So, we'll need to ensure your Prospect understands the gravity of the situation and possesses the confidence and skills to address the problem(s).

VI. Explore Areas of Suspected Weakness

Like the above, where we addressed some of the critical factors of the assignment, we want to understand any limitations this Prospect might bring to the company. For example, are they too soft on potential problem employees? Do they need to improve communication with their team, peers, or management? Do they carry their weight and walk the talk? Are there any significant failures or missteps to their credit? What is the Prospect's reputation within their industry?

When discussing a weakness with the Prospect, it's essential to approach the conversation with empathy. It's imperative to discuss any defects or limitations to understand how the prospect has encountered challenges and whether they resolved the issue and learned from it.

It's always appropriate to assume positive intent during such conversations as long as the facts come out, and they usually do. You can inquire if the Prospect is actively working to address any limitations; they should be able to provide specific examples, including seeking feedback or training to improve.

VII. Define Additional Details of the Assignment if Prospect is on Target

If there are any factors that we did not share with the Prospect by this time, client permitting, we would then share that confidential information once the client and recruiter agree to do so. Clients may allow you to share such details with a select Prospect or two as an incentive. At times, an NDA would be required.

VIII. Comparison to Search Specification

All your Prospects will display differing strengths and limitations while meeting or exceeding the Must Haves. Apply a certain percentage weight to each Must Have and rank-order them relative to their impact on the job and company.

With a unique, in-person presence, especially for sales and marketing roles, physical demeanor, presentation, and appearance have an impact. Perhaps the client might prefer a Prospect that displays phenomenal stage presence over someone with a few additional years of experience in the client's industry but lacks the outgoing personality required, for example.

Once your client reads your future Candidate letter, they can decide to what degree any minor shortcoming could become a factor.

IX. Development of Additional Prospects/Source

To what degree you keep searching for additional Sources and Prospects is up to you. Still, there should always be some activity on the sourcing side until you have two to three solid Candidates you plan to meet yourself. Preferably, a few additionally interested and qualified Prospects who came close in quality and you're remaining in contact with them.

Keep trying to reach everyone your research led you to. After all, you took the time to identify them, so follow through.

X. Tentative Arrangements for Personal Meetings or Sign-off

For the Prospect(s) you've confirmed meet most of the skills you're seeking, and both client and Prospect remain interested, you'll arrange face-to-face meetings with them.

You will also eventually get to the point where interested and qualified Prospects will not be moving forward in the search for any number of reasons, including the simple fact that you have other Prospects that are more qualified. As discussed, we do need other Prospects in the queue in case the primary Prospects you meet or Candidates you present to your client implode for any reason: poor references, a misrepresentation on their resume, a change of heart, or a Candidate meets your client but fails to impress.

Be honest in telling them that you appreciate the interest and time they've invested with you and that you'd like to remain in contact. They could still become a terrific source, if not a Prospect themselves on a future assignment. Don't waste the time you've invested in this individual. I cannot tell you how often those relationships have bene-fitted the individual and me.

XI. Repeat Prospect Development to Assure Broad Industry Coverage

Once you've found those qualified Prospects you plan to meet, don't rest on your laurels. Instead, as implied above, take one additional look and follow up on any promising leads you could not reach before. Turn over every rock relative to other companies, vertical markets, associations, startups, etc., and look into them. Not to be flippant, but it's true: sometimes, some of the best Prospects and Candidates are found in one of the last places you look.

Bottom line, as a best practice, assuming resources and supports exist within the search firm, recruiters should continue searching for Prospects even after recruiting three exceptional Prospects for several reasons. One, as already discussed, is backup Prospects. So, if you need backup Prospects, keep looking. Another reason is that there may be future hiring needs even if you've filled the current position. Building a pipeline of Sources and Prospects for future roles can save time and effort when the time comes to begin another search.

Yet another reason to keep searching is that it allows the recruiter to increase the diversity of their Candidate pool and ensure they reach a more comprehensive range of Candidates. Keep in mind that continuing to search for Candidates allows the recruiter to test new recruiting strategies and see what works best for their organization.

XII. Comparison of Individual Prospects to each other and Search Specification

Take the rest of the Prospects you wish to develop and complete these in-depth phone interviews to determine whom you should meet with in person. We'll rank-order our Prospects and ensure that the most robust and qualified are prioritized when scheduling your face-to-face interviews.

XIII. Prepare Prospect Strength/ Weakness Lists

Put together a rank-ordered list of Must Haves, other skills looked for, and limitations on each Prospect. Probe all areas during these second phone interviews and revisit the subject if meeting in person. If your Prospect demonstrated significant burdens at this search stage, we likely should have identified them earlier.

XIV. Prepare Arrangements for Prospect Meetings and Candidate Development Phase

You and your client may have agreed to discuss these Prospects before you travel to meet those selected, incurring additional time and expense. Regardless, work with the Prospect to secure travel and hotel. Have them forward receipts to you for reimbursement for their costs incurred.

These meetings will set the stage for determining who will meet with your client. Therefore, once you (and perhaps your client) have agreed and decided upon who is qualified for you to meet, you will elevate each of these Prospects to Candidate status and make arrangements for your face-to-face interviews.

XV. Prepare Sign-off Letter to Prospects not Meeting Total Search Requirements

Concurrent with your in-person interviews, you must close some loops and communicate with those Prospects you have decided not to pursue.

If an individual expresses interest but differs from what the client is looking for, we need to be straightforward and sincere with each. We'll re-label them as a Source (if they've referred someone or suggested other helpful information) and a Prospect-X for this search. Flagging these folks with two labels will allow you to bring up Sources who were less than qualified for this assignment but may be of benefit on similar future searches. This process lays the groundwork for an honest and open relationship from which you, both recruiter and Prospect, can benefit.

A gentle reminder: By checking in periodically with your client throughout the search process and keeping them updated about the search's status, you're also validating that your approach is on the right track. Thus, your client gains added faith in your firm and you.

4

SEARCH METHODOLOGY

D: THE CANDIDATE DEVELOPMENT PHASE

This chapter focuses on your face-to-face interviews with your most promising Prospects, now elevated to Candidate status. This stage is particularly significant and exciting as it allows you to observe the Candidates in person. It also provides an opportunity to gather additional information that may have been missed or limited during earlier stages of the process. During these interviews, you can assess their personal brand, communication style, demeanor, stature and bearing, listening skills, and any unique quirks they may have.

Use probing questions to guide the Prospects in providing detailed responses. Probing questions help extract specific information and allows you to align the interview topics with your client's needs. Here are just a few examples of probing questions that can be used:

- What were the specific results or outcomes of a particular situation?
- Who did your actions impact: customers, employees, and/or stakeholders?
- What resources were available to address the problem, and how effectively were they utilized?
- How supportive were the company and management during this process?

By incorporating these probing questions and others, you can ensure the Prospects provide detailed and comprehensive responses that showcase their abilities, problem-solving skills, and the impact they had in their previous roles.

In the Candidate letter to your client, it is essential to highlight the Candidate's current and previous roles, delving into how their day-to-day responsibilities align with the Must Haves. Go over examples of their achievements, challenges, and problem-solving abilities. To evaluate their experiences effectively, encourage the Prospects to use the STAR method when answering behavioral interview questions.

This basic method involves discussing the Situation, Task, Action, and Result of their past experiences.

My Candidate letters were typically story-like, summarizing essential information about their character from youth on, how their upbringing affected their growth, then tested in college and early career life, through to the present. I've also written summaries detailing the Candidate's life, starting from the present and working backward, as with resumes. My preference was to begin from my early years in college, followed by an enviable period of professional growth.

When I initially started meeting Candidates, I found that using face-to-face interviews for collecting further detailed career information was less productive than I had desired. I used too much of my time with the Candidate on career facts and specifics that I overlooked in our previous phone interviews. I realized I needed more time observing and probing to add the human dimension to my written presentation.

I was spending most of my meetings jotting down responsibilities across various jobs. I realized I needed to be more observant of whether the Candidate was personable, approachable, engaged, a good listener, had a distracting habit, etc. As referred to in the previous chapter, clients with whom you have a relatively new relationship may prefer you discuss which Prospects stood out from your in-depth phone interviews and with whom you want to interview face-to-face (the topic of this chapter) before arranging interviews with your client company (next chapter). Because you're spending your client's money to interview Candidates in person, and your relationship is such that you are entrusted with determining whom to meet, you'll need to ensure your client meets with only those with the required skill set and background experience. For this reason, it's preferred that the recruiter maintain ongoing communication with the client.

In our next chapter, we'll discuss arranging Candidate/client interviews once the client has approved your choices and read your three-to-five-page comprehensive background letters.

Remember: when meeting Prospects in person, set the tone and pace for the interview as you evaluate overall presentation and demeanor. Notice how they conduct themselves in an interview setting, if it appears they have done some further research on your client (assuming we've shared their identity), whether they ask appropriate questions, and whether they are forthcoming in their responses (or haphazard and evasive). You want to feel proud and excited to present such an individual to your client and understand why.

Okay, we've narrowed the field and gained consensus with our client relative to which Candidates we will meet in person. We'll share more details about the role and organization (to the degree you are permitted) upon meeting.

I would hold meetings in as few cities as possible and fly Candidates to me, interviewing at least three to eight individuals per trip. Face-to-face meetings with Candidates are typically arranged by the search firm, who, in turn, reimburses the Prospects and invoices the client. If the Candidate made their own travel arrangements, ensure they are reimbursed within a reasonable period of time.

Interviews can be held anywhere but typically in hotel rooms, hotel restaurants, or even sitting areas, as long as any venue is relatively private and quiet. You'll also experience clandestine meetings with Candidates who do not want to be seen locally or have some other reason for proactively maintaining confidentiality, such as a well-known figure with a direct competitor.

D: THE CANDIDATE DEVELOPMENT PHASE

I. Personal Meetings with Qualified Candidates

You're now sitting down with your Candidate in a private setting where you are not overheard, and there are no interruptions, except for perhaps a waitstaff member.

Remember your purpose. You're the gatekeeper and recruiting executive on a confidential mission to discuss an opportunity that could conceivably change the lives of your Candidate and their family while enhancing the value of your client, aka your Candidate's new employer.

Unless discussed in advance, preferably, dress in business attire (suit and tie) or, at minimum, a sports jacket and dress shirt. Wear appropriate clothes depending upon the industry; for example, entertainment executives often dress in business casual, while attorneys tend to dress more professionally. Observe the same of your Prospect. Did they notice what kind of impression they would create regardless of whether they were dressed in a business suit or casual? Are their clothes clean and pressed, or did it appear as if they paid little attention to the impression they would make?

II. Detail Analysis of Professional Profile - College to Present, Plus Develop Reference Listing, Total Organization Analysis, Responsibilities and Performance, Accomplishments/Failures, Compensation History, etc.

Reference Listing

- *List of references. See Chapter 5 for more detail.*

Total Organization Analysis

- You'll want to walk away from this meeting with a solid understanding of where your candidate resides within their organization.

Responsibilities and Performance

- Detail precisely their scope of responsibility and impact on the business with that authority.
- Gather verifiable facts to validate the positive and negative impact on your Candidate's business.
- What skills do they bring to your client that parallel the Must Haves of the assignment?

Accomplishments/Failures

- Detail their wins, their percentage of contribution to those wins, and the results.
- What worked and didn't, and when things did not, why not, and how did they get fixed?
- Probe in detail relative to setbacks and failures. Whose participation contributed to that loss? The Candidate? A subordinate?

Compensation History, etc.

- Asking compensation questions can be tricky for the rare Candidate who feels it's too early to ask invasive personal questions.
- Frankly, we should have some perspective by now; otherwise, we shouldn't be considering the candidate.
- If discussing compensation components is an issue, explain that your conversations are confidential and that you hope to see both career and compensation progression. You need to

confirm that we are still in the comp ballpark should an offer be made.
- Make sure to consider all unique components of their current compensation package.
- Do they clearly understand the job and what your client aims to achieve?
- Do they possess the necessary experience and confidence to accomplish the tasks now and in the future? Do they convey a belief in their ability to succeed?
- Does any skill, patent, confidential, proprietary, or inside information connected to their current or prior employer(s) exist that could cause problems should they leave their company and become employed by your client?

During the face-to-face interview, there will come the point where you will determine that a Candidate aligns with most, if not all, of the desired qualifications. Remember, considering all the data you've collected immediately before and during this interview, you've decided to advance their candidacy and proceed to meet them for yourself. Then, if the facts and your intuition tell you they are viable for the next step of meeting your client, you'll develop the three-to-five-page letter describing the Candidate's journey from college to the present. If the Candidate has notable accomplishments from their youth, it can be worthwhile to highlight them in the background summary.

While delving into the details of the Candidate's recent positions, seek insights into the dynamics of their organization(s), mainly focusing on the past 5-6 years, regardless of the number of titles held during that period. What were significant accomplishments, what prompted any promotions, what were/are their areas of responsibility, and were/were management's expectations met?

Once again, it is essential to walk through the organizational charts of your Candidate's current and previous positions. Confirm *exactly* where your Candidate is placed within the business, identify titles (and, if possible, names) of individuals above, at the same level, and report to your Candidate; at minimum, confirm job titles if your Candidate is uncomfortable sharing a name.

Don't be shy when inquiring about their working relationships with individuals on their org chart. You're having a confidential conversation and are not there to pilfer the identities of teammates. Instead, your sole purpose at this time is to gain insight into your Candidate's current organizational dynamics. It may well become impactful for client presentations, especially if, for example, a stressful turnaround was particularly challenging, or a couple of coworkers were difficult to work with or manage, etc.

Record the titles and names identified during these conversations in your organizational chart program.

Finally, gain an understanding of the Candidate's current physical work environment in comparison to the requirements of your client. For example, do they primarily work in an office, remotely, or a combination of both?

III. Detail Personal Profile

During your first face-to-face meeting with Candidates, it is crucial to observe their conduct, appearance, and communication skills while considering the specific position they are interviewing for. For instance, a sales executive role may require a confident appearing Candidate with an affable and outgoing communication style; remain on high alert for evidence of these qualities.

Pay attention to how engaged and interested the Candidate appears during the meeting. Do they maintain eye contact or tend to look away? Are they actively listening and responding? Evaluate whether they ask thoughtful questions that demonstrate their research on your client. Notice if they change their seated positions throughout the conversation and assess whether they appear relaxed yet fully attentive.

As important as it is to collect relevant information, it's crucial to do so without asking illegal or uncomfortable questions. Again, ask if any aspects of the job may hurt the Candidate's family members. For example, inquire about factors such as a longer commute, potential relocation, or extended travel periods while ensuring the questions remain appropriate and respectful.

Between your minimum of two phone calls and a face-to-face interview with your Candidate, you've gathered enough background information to create your Candidate's 3–5-page background letter. In the document, address their stature and bearing, their conversational style, whether they are relaxed yet personable, whether they are listening or often looking away, whether they were engaged, and whether you observed any other unique attributes or limitations during your face-to-face interview.

In addition to any likely family concerns, including relocation, we continue to look for any new or potential future obstacle(s) that may prevent the Candidate from accepting the post. These questions are not meant to be invasive. They play a vital role in the process for the Candidate and encourage a deeper consideration of the role and logistics.

IV. Compare Charisma Match with Client

You don't necessarily need a psychology degree to know if someone would be a good match. Since you've already met with both Candidate and the client, take what you've observed and consider whether their personalities and communication styles would meld. Does your Candidate demonstrate enthusiasm about your client company's culture, mission, and goals? Would your Candidate work well with their new boss and peers?

Depending upon your client's resources and various other considerations, companies may utilize the services of an outside consultant or firm that conducts personality tests like the Myers-Briggs Type Indicator (MBTI), DiSC Assessment, StrengthsFinder, and Predictive

Index. In my experience, they were only utilized for very senior positions and, in one scenario, for the core team of a startup.

V. Explore Details of Suspect Areas of Concern and Critical Requirements

During your Candidate meetings, you should have their trust to confidentially address any concerns or issues your Candidate may have with your client or the role, as it could be consequential. This is an opportunity to discuss potential dealbreakers that have emerged recently. For instance, references might expose one Candidate to multiple negative interactions or disciplinary actions at one of their employers. Other factors to consider include geographical constraints, compensation expectations, or timing-related matters that are not directly job-related, such as an ill family member or relative.

By openly communicating these concerns with your client, you can collaboratively assess whether these issues are critical and if they would significantly impact the suitability of a particular Candidate for the role.

VI. Decision: Candidate, Sign-off, or Hold in Abeyance

As you begin to interview Candidates, you will likely identify those that are qualified and ready to meet with your client. Gauge not only your Candidate's availability but that of your client; control everyone's schedule to the best of your ability. Ideally, three candidates would meet with your client within the seven-to-ten-day window, but that's not always possible. Yet we would like all eligible candidates to meet your client without stretching out your timeline and possibly having something go sideways.

On the one hand, for those Candidates with whom you've decided are not moving forward, it is essential to conclude the dialogue properly. Express to them that this is just the beginning of your relationship and that you hope to stay in touch and provide mutual support to one another.

But consider this: before this face-to-face interview, you've invested at least two long phone calls with this individual. What did you identify during your in-person meeting that was not evident on those phone calls? What did you fail to probe? What clues were missed that only surfaced when you got together? Was it something only apparent by being in the presence of the Candidate?

As for the remaining Prospects, some are not as strong as others. In this case, instead of informing them that their candidacy will be put on hold temporarily, suggest to these Candidates, as mentioned earlier, that the client has decided to interview others first but asked that we refrain from turning anyone off at this time. After those interviews, the client may choose to interview additional Candidates. Assure them that you will periodically reach out and update them regarding their candidacy.

If it is necessary to sign off a Candidate, be honest with them but provide helpful feedback. This is a legitimate part of our process, aiming to pursue the most qualified Candidates without disqualifying any otherwise suitable Candidates until a final decision is made. Keeping all Candidates motivated is crucial while avoiding overselling the possibility of interviewing with the client.

For any rock-solid Candidate who fails to get the job, attempt to maintain a constructive relationship. Let them know you will always be receptive to their calls and that you will stay alert to any future searches that may be a fit for them. Ask them to update you with any changes in their phone number or email. Since meeting them, you've learned that their track record and skill set are enviable, and their industry insight is unique. Get an updated sense of what kind of opportunity they would be interested in and if you may occasionally reach out to discuss such a job. You would be interested in investing the time to have subsequent conversations off-record.

You would also appreciate their permission to occasionally call and share details about future confidential searches and learn if they know someone who might benefit from hearing more about them. Keep it positive and professional.

VII. Discuss Details of Client Assignment, Organization, and Environment without Identification of Client

Is it possible that, until now, your client has insisted on maintaining their confidentiality? In that case, you described the company in generic terms while sharing job-specific details at length (i.e., responsibilities, resources available, expected results of the new hire, culture, growth plans, and desired skill set).

If you have yet to reveal your client's identity by this time, and since you've determined one or more Candidates should meet your client, you're likely free to identify them by now. The only other requirement that your client may have requested would be to have your Candidate sign an NDA before you reveal their identity.

Finish by informing the Candidate of any additional details of the assignment yet to be shared.

VIII. Obtain Expression of Interest

Though we've periodically asked for confirmation of interest, we must confirm that no last-minute obstacles have manifested during the recruitment process.

Ideally, the Candidate continues to confirm there are no impediments that would affect them from meeting your client and accepting the job if offered (assuming the offer was within the Candidate's expectations). Share your enthusiasm for their candidacy and look for anything less than 100% commitment.

IX. Identify the Client Once Approved

Once you've decided to move forward with a Candidate, if not revealed already, reveal their identity now.

Respecting your client's preference for maintaining confidentiality during a retained search is essential. For various reasons, a client may want to keep the circle of people aware of the search process relatively small. One reason is to prevent the search from being leaked to local or national press and newscasters, industry websites, and publications, all of which have the power to raise concerns about the company's stability or create unnecessary speculation. Another reason could be the presence of an incumbent employee in the role who is unaware of the discreet search being conducted.

As a professional in the search process, it is crucial to always comply with your client's requests regarding confidentiality. By doing so, you uphold their trust and ensure that the search proceeds in a manner that aligns with their specific needs and concerns. |

X. Discuss Details of Client Assignment, Environment, and Personalities

At this stage, we will provide our Candidates with a deeper insight into our client's organization. This includes sharing more intimate details about the client's business, a comprehensive understanding of the position, the reasons behind the search, and the client's current needs and challenges. We will also highlight the organizational culture and the personalities of management and peers within the company.

XI. Obtain Schedule of Candidate Availability for Future Meetings with Client

Ideally, it would be best to know when the client will be available to interview Candidates. It is essential to encourage your Candidates to conduct a thorough amount of research about the firm beforehand and be prepared to ask thoughtful questions. This demonstrates their business acumen and showcases their genuine interest in the opportunity. This will enable them to engage in meaningful discussions during the interview process and make a favorable impression on the Client. Demonstrating knowledge about the firm and a sincere interest in the position will increase their chances of success in the recruitment process.

XII. Preparation of Documentation Presenting Details of Professional and Personal History to Client

Once you have finished interviewing selected Candidates, it's time to create the three-to-five-page Candidate letter we've referred to multiple times for each Candidate you plan to present to your client.

See the Appendix for examples of Candidate letters.

In this detailed letter, strive to provide a comprehensive and engaging account of the Candidate's background, including their education, employment history, any employment gaps, and how they align with the requirements set by your client.

Illustrate how the Candidate possesses the necessary personal and professional skills and relevant experience for the position. Emphasize their unique qualities and demonstrate how they fit within your client's company and the specific role.

With the background information you've collected on the first two calls and your face-to-face, you have been encouraged to keep data orderly and formatted so creating a historical summary of your Candidate's life and career will be straightforward. Order your interview questions in a way that facilitates the creation of the Candidate letter efficiently. Typically, it should take no more than a couple of hours to compose each letter. As you gain experience, it takes less time. Consider utilizing voice recognition technology to dictate and create a timeline of the Candidate's accomplishments.

Provide all the relevant facts and accomplishments but present the information in a manner that generates excitement and interest from your Client. Showcase the Candidate's career trajectory and achievements in a way that captures your Client's attention and motivates them to want to meet.

XIII. Preparation of Candidate Comparative Analysis for Client

Arrange to speak or meet with your client and discuss your mutual impressions of the Candidates presented. Help decide who will interview your client and when.

We want to offer an honest assessment, compare each Candidate's background to the position description, and balance that with your impressions upon meeting in person. Whenever possible, submit your Candidates within a reasonable window of time from each other. Present them in whichever order you want, although I've prescribed to the theory of presenting my second-best Candidate first, my best Candidate second, and my least-qualified Candidate (of the three) third.

5

SEARCH METHODOLOGY

E: ASSIGNMENT COMPLETION PHASE

After conducting face-to-face meetings with all viable Prospects, you have reached the final stage of the Search Methodology. With a strong belief in a select number of remaining Candidates, it's time to formally present them to your client through a comprehensive Candidate letter and subsequent communication.

Ideally, though not always possible, you should aim to identify no more than three individuals to be given to your client and assist with interview arrangements; more Candidates only confuse the selection process. Seek feedback from your client on each Candidate and promptly address any negatives or concerns. Please pay attention to your client's level of interest in each Candidate, compare it to their ranking after the interviews, and establish a timeframe for further discussions with your client.

As the recruiter, it is helpful to be fully aware of if not directly involved in, the travel arrangements to your client's offices, which is typically the process at this stage.

Additionally, it is highly beneficial to confirm that your Candidate has the interview schedule once you receive it. Share your impressions of the people they will meet, including their personalities, communication styles, and other unique characteristics. Hopefully, you gathered this data during your initial client meeting, as described in Chapter 1.

Now, let's pause for a moment and reflect upon each Candidate's journey to this point, as well as yours:

You've invested an efficient and effectual effort in early-stage conversations with Prospects, venturing into a broader yet more intimate dialog by expanding upon their background through extended phone interviews followed by your meetings with Candidates, then narrowing the field when presenting the best Candidates to your client.

Your return on investment more often trends positively as you interview and present only the most qualified Candidates to your client.

As we reach out and, in effect, change peoples' lives, each step becomes more crucial and consequential. Remember that your reputation and efficacy are always on stage and in front of your clients, Sources, and Candidates, with increasing impact at each stage of the Search Methodology.

Let's proceed to the last section of the Search Methodology, the Assignment Completion Phase. This marks a critical point in the process, where everything is about to pay off as you facilitate the upcoming interview by supporting the Candidate and client in making further progress.

E. ASSIGNMENT COMPLETION PHASE

I. Meeting with Client – Review and Analysis of Candidates with Consultant Recommendations

Once your client has read your Candidate summary letters, arrange to discuss the letter with your client once they've digested them.

Listen carefully to their feedback and any concerns. Be prepared to respond with your thoughts and impressions and why you strongly believe your client should meet a specific Candidate for an in-person interview. Emphasize your preferences and reasoning. Once you agree on a path forward, arrange for the Candidate(s) to meet the client, usually at their offices. Even if the client makes all the travel arrangements, stay vigilant and communicate with both parties until the interview day and the Candidate shows up. We'll want to avoid any break in communication that might lead to a disruption of the interview. This cannot be emphasized enough.

II. Establish Dates for the Meeting between the client and Candidate

Identify your client's preferred interview process and available interview dates and confirm availability with your Candidate. It's preferable if both Candidate and the client are flexible in their availability, which can be affected by the absence of one or more interviewers or other circumstances.

Understand the meeting's format, such as how many people will be interviewing your Candidate and physically where the interviews will take place. Ask for a list of interviewers, the interview schedule, and any pertinent background information you should be aware of regarding these individuals.

You may need to handle almost all the interview arrangements, similar to your face-to-face interviews. At the same time, in other situations, the client may have designated an individual in their HR department to handle these logistics. On rare occasions, the Candidate may make arrangements with the client to cover the associated costs through reimbursement.

As mentioned earlier, consider it essential to address any concerns or issues your Candidate may have before the interview. Keep in touch until they have traveled to your client's location for the scheduled meetings. Ensure all necessary preparations are in place to facilitate a smooth and successful interview process.

III. Contact Candidate to Arrange Time and Location of Meeting

Connect with your Candidate, advise them of your client's availability, and confirm that their availability matches your client's. Unless the interviews are local or within reasonable driving distance, Candidates often travel by airplane and stay overnight in preparation for interviews during a significant part of the following day.

While schedules are dynamic and often change, at times, either the client or Candidate may need to be rescheduled. However, my mindset has always been to err on my client's side. Unless your Candidate has a solid, valid reason to reschedule, I will look for effort on their part to attempt to reorganize their schedule to meet your client's availability. When scheduling client interviews, and there are conflicts, such as the same-day availability between two Candidates, always prioritize your stronger Candidate.

IV. Confirmation of Client-Candidate Meeting

Maintaining communication with all parties at this juncture is essential. It's best to connect by phone, preferably to hear their voice and tone; otherwise, email or text your Candidates within 48 hours of their departure to the client. It's a reasonable gesture as you want to confirm they have everything they need for their trips (i.e., itinerary, directions, hotel reservation information, client's address, and phone number). The day before, confirm with the client that meetings are set, and that everything has remained the same since your last communication.

V. First/Multiple Meetings

The client has met each Candidate (let's say three Candidates, for simplicity's sake). After each interview, you'll want to communicate with the Candidate and the client. It's preferable to pre-arrange a time to talk to your Candidate to avoid playing telephone tag. Then when you speak to your client afterward, you'll be able to share your Candidates' feedback, and the dialog with be more productive relative to any concerns that may have surfaced.

I must reinforce the suggestion of prearranging a time to call the Candidate once they are comfortable and can speak freely, such as back at their hotel or airport lounge while waiting for their return flight. Once reached, ask about any meeting highlights, what, if any, concerns need to be addressed, and, indeed, their current level of interest.

With both client and Candidate, ensure you maintain confidentiality where necessary.

Here are just a sampling of questions you could ask your Candidate:

- How do you feel the interview went?
- Did you feel comfortable with those interviewing you?
- What were some questions they asked you?

- How did you respond to these questions?
- Were there any questions that you found challenging to answer?
- What are your impressions of the company and the role after the interview?
- Did you have any concerns or questions following the interview?
- Do you think that your skills and experiences were understood and valued?
- Were there any highlights of the interview(s)?
- Is there anything you wish you had said differently or added?
- Did you learn anything new about the company or role that excites you?
- Did the interview change your interest in the position or company? If so, how?
- How well do you think the role matches your skills and interests?
- On a scale of 1 to 10, how interested are you in the position after the interview?
- Did your client give you an indication of next steps or when you might hear back?
- Would you be interested in moving forward if they chose to proceed?

Here are just a sampling of questions you could ask your client:

- How do you feel the interview went?
- Did the Candidate demonstrate the necessary skills and experience for the role?
- How did the Candidate's personality fit with the company culture and team dynamic?
- Were there any red flags or areas of concern?
- What were the Candidate's strengths and weaknesses in the interview?

- Did the Candidate show a strong understanding of the role and its requirements?
- Did the candidate ask insightful questions?
- Based on the interview, how well would the candidate perform in this role?
- How do you see them fitting into the company's future growth?
- Are you considering moving forward with a second interview or job offer?
- What are the next steps in the process, and when can we expect a decision?
- Are there any additional skills or traits you'd like to explore in a second interview?
- On a scale of 1-10, how would you rate the candidate's fit for the role based on this interview?

These questions can provide valuable insights to the recruiter and help both parties determine the next steps. The recruiter can give feedback to the candidate, assist in improving subsequent interviews, or help facilitate the following stages of the hiring process.

VI. Client Interest Expressed - Detail Reference Check Made with Understanding of Candidate. This is Done in Majority of Cases to Protect Security of Candidate's Current Assignment

The client has met all Candidates and expressed strong interest in one (our best Candidate who interviewed second), provided good feedback on another (our first Candidate interview), and showed limited interest in the third Candidate (the last interview). The object now is to motivate the top two Candidates to continue the process without any fallout until a decision is made.

Your client advised you that they would consider either of the first two Candidates met and would like to get feedback from both Candidates, including their level of interest at this point.

We now need to run references. I typically will ask for two to three individuals to whom each Candidate has reported in the past, two to three peers, and at least a couple of subordinates. Additionally, during interviews, I would have already asked if our candidate had ever terminated anyone, and if so, I would like to get one or two names in that regard. This latter request often provides me with tremendous insight into the candidate.

Reference checks are a vital part of the hiring process that allows recruiters to gain insight into Candidates and their work style, strengths, weaknesses, and past performance. Here are some excellent questions that the recruiter could ask for each type of reference.

Former Superiors:

- Can you confirm the Candidate's job title, responsibilities, and employment dates while at your company?
- How did the Candidate contribute to team objectives and company goals?
- Can you describe the candidate's reliability, punctuality, and ability to meet deadlines?
- What are their strengths and areas that could use improvement?
- In what areas did the candidate excel?
- How did the Candidate handle feedback and criticism?
- Would you rehire this Candidate if given the opportunity?

Former Peers:

- How would you describe the Candidate's teamwork skills?
- How did the Candidate handle conflict or disagreement with team members?
- What is it like working with this person daily?
- Can you provide an example of a project where the Candidate particularly excelled?
- What is the Candidate reliable and trustworthy?

- Did the Candidate take responsibility when they made a mistake or misspoke?

Former Subordinates:

- How would you describe the Candidate's management or leadership style?
- How did the Candidate foster a positive and productive work environment?
- Can you provide an example where the Candidate demonstrated exemplary leadership skills?
- How does the Candidate handle feedback and criticism?
- Did the Candidate support your professional development? If so, how?

An individual that the Candidate had terminated:

- Can you share the circumstances that led to your termination? *(Be sensitive here as this could be a very delicate topic)*
- How did the Candidate handle your termination process?
- How did they communicate feedback on your performance before the termination? Were you given a chance to improve?
- Can you describe the Candidate's fairness and professionalism throughout this process?
- Would you work with this individual again, given different circumstances?

When sharing your references' research with your client, remember that each reference's comfort level, the nature of their relationship with the Candidate, and legal restrictions might influence the level of detail they can provide. It's important to ask open-ended questions that allow the reference to share their unique perspective on the candidates, their skills, and their performance.

These names were given to you in complete confidence by your candidates, and the expectation is that you will be discreet and firmly advise each reference that their discretion is also appreciated. To protect our Candidates' confidentiality, upon speaking to each reference, I would recommend telling them that the Candidate is gainfully employed; however, we discreetly approached them with a unique opportunity. They have not committed to anything but agreed to remain open-minded and listen to our proposal. The Candidate agreed we could call their references to get a general impression of our Candidate.

If I received a tepid response about my Candidate from any reference, I would ask them if they knew anyone who might be stronger than our current Candidate. I have only asked that question a few times, and on one or two occasions, I was led to additional Sources and Prospects. Still, sadly, only one Candidate-level individual was ever identified.

Place the business-related references in your organizational chart program as you would any other Source or referral during each search. Add titles, companies, and additional information about the reference's job history if you have it as you conduct Candidate references. While we do not want to abuse these brief relationships, don't hesitate to contact them as a Source in the future, reference your original reference call, and gauge the degree they cooperate.

Interesting results can arise from performing references. I called one reference for a president search I was conducting; the reference was the chief executive of a $20B publicly held healthcare corporation. When I was finished referencing his former business peer, the chief executive asked me how we came to earn the search; my firm was a boutique business, not a large global search firm, and he had not heard of us. I replied that the client who hired us saw value because we only work with one client in each industry we serve, giving us the freedom to recruit from anyone in that sphere. That incentive resulted in a future vice-presidential search and a new client.

VII. Critique with Both Client and Candidate of Details of Interest and Questionable Factors

After the interviews have concluded and references documented, call the client first. Pull everything together: your Candidate letters, professional insight, reference feedback, and your client's impressions after the interviews. It would be best if you walked away from that call knowing what the pluses and minuses were from the client's point of view of each Candidate. Which Candidate is of greater interest to your client and why?

Then reach out to your Candidate and share appropriate feedback. Be straight with your Candidates and let them know where they stand in the client's eyes. But before you call, place yourself in their shoes and think for a few minutes about how to share the feedback, positive or negative. Regardless, this is no time to turn off any Candidate that has met your client until an offer is made and accepted. It's rare, but decisions about making an offer and to whom can change overnight.

VIII. Client Meeting/Decision to Act on First Candidate of Interest

You and your client discussed the results of each Candidate's interview and the reference notes. Now the client has decided to make an offer.

All this time, we have been communicating with our three Candidate(s), keeping them warm and interested.

It is often, at this point, before an offer is made, that the client or recruiter will verify college degrees and any other certifications claimed by the Candidate, all with the permission of the Candidate.

IX. Discussion of Compensation Offer with Client

Engage thoroughly with your client regarding the compensation package they plan to offer the Candidate. You're confident that throughout your discussions, your Candidate has been consistent when divulging their current compensation level and has provided their expectations regarding the new assignment's remuneration. If you've maintained an open dialog with your client relative to each Candidate's current and anticipated compensation, you should expect the proposed offer to align with their expectations. Discuss and identify areas of flexibility for both parties, such as stock grants, yearly bonuses, relocation assistance, and other relevant factors.

Maintain an open line of communication with your client throughout the process, ensuring that any potential issues or concerns related to compensation are promptly addressed. Understanding the Candidate's compensation expectations well before the last minute is important. Have these conversations early on, while they are still in the Prospect stage before they become an official Candidate. Proactively discussing compensation can avoid misunderstandings and facilitate a smoother negotiation process.

As an executive recruiter, you are pivotal in facilitating a mutually beneficial relationship between the client and a potential hire. Negotiating a salary can be delicate, requiring a balance of diplomacy and business acumen. Every negotiation is unique and requires a tailored approach. As an executive recruiter. reputation and future business prospects depend on successful placements, where both parties feel they've received a fair deal. Your main goal is to ensure the client and Candidate are satisfied with the outcome.

Several tactics can be utilized when helping a client and a newly hired executive to agree on a salary.

- Provide informed advice to both parties. Given the market and the client's constraints, let the Candidate know if their expectations are realistic. Similarly, advise the client if their offer is likely to be seen as competitive. Sometimes, if the base salary can't be increased due to company policies or budgets, you can suggest creative ways to enhance the compensation package. This could be a signing bonus, relocation expenses, or enhanced perks and benefits.

- Promote open and honest communication, helping both sides understand each other's expectations and constraints. For instance, the client's budget and the candidate's salary expectations should be conveyed to ensure understanding.
- Sometimes, it may be beneficial to negotiate the terms individually instead of presenting the whole package at once. This allows for give-and-take on individual components without derailing the entire negotiation.
- Encourage both parties to prepare to compromise. The company might consider meeting the Candidate's demands if the executive is perfect for the role. Or a lower base salary offer could be offset by additional equity, as an example.
- Once an agreement is reached, ensure it is appropriately documented and both parties are satisfied with the outcome.
- The recruiter can assist by emphasizing the candidate's value and potential contributions to the company. Specific experiences, skills, and qualifications should be highlighted to justify the salary.
- If the client cannot meet the candidate's salary expectations immediately, the recruiter could discuss the potential for future raises or promotions based on performance.
- To prevent the negotiation from becoming adversarial, the recruiter can foster a collaborative atmosphere, presenting the negotiation as a problem-solving exercise rather than a zero-sum game.
- Once an agreement is reached, the recruiter should ensure that all agreed-upon terms are included in the formal job offer. The recruiter should be available for follow-up discussions in case of any questions or concerns.

X. Client Offer to Candidate

In most cases, the client will extend the job offer to the final Candidate. I have no preference either way. There are supportive arguments for and negatives regarding who makes the offer.

However, I have been fortunate to work with many exceptional clients in this regard, so there was less concern on my part, especially if additional negotiating needs to occur.

That said, once the offer is made, promptly contact your client first to gather feedback on the Candidate's reaction and whether the offer has been accepted. If the offer has yet to be accepted, it is crucial to determine the delay.

XI. Candidate Contacts with Consultant

After speaking with your client, communicate with the Candidate and get their perception of the offer. Either you will congratulate them on their new role, or you will be informed they are not ready to decide for any number of reasons, such as when specific issues in the offer are addressed or clarified. Or it could be that the Candidate may need to consult with their spouse or attorney. You must effectively navigate the situation, provide the necessary support, and promptly address any outstanding issues.

Your role here is to ensure your client and Candidate are in communication and checking off every bullet point of the offer. Most importantly, you'll want to ensure everyone is happy, excited, optimistic, and focused on making the transition successful and stress-free.

XII. Candidate Acceptance Direct to Client

While you may know that the Candidate will accept the offer, the Candidate should communicate directly with the client.

Before making an offer, I've often guided my client to enhance one or more elements of the offer slightly higher than the Candidate's expectations, which often leads to successful acceptance. This can include increasing a sign-on bonus or adjusting equity based on personal and corporate performance.

However, there have been instances where Candidates anticipated an offer and became overly demanding, requiring me to manage their expectations accordingly.

Although striving to understand Candidates' expectations in advance, there may be occasions where their expectations change, albeit rarely. If a Candidate wishes to negotiate directly with the client after receiving the offer, I have found the following steps helpful when advising Candidates on how to proceed:

- Understand the position and location dynamics and be prepared to adjust expectations accordingly. Determine the bare minimum you will accept and discuss these expectations in advance.
- When negotiating with your new employer, express your appreciation for the offer and provide concrete examples to support why you deserve higher compensation.
- Listen to the employer's perspective and be flexible, just as you expect them to be.
- Understand their point of view and engage in constructive dialogue.
- If the initial salary offer cannot be increased to the Candidate's desired amount, consider alternative benefits such as additional paid time off, flexible working arrangements, or professional development opportunities.

To repeat, once an agreement is reached, ensure that the terms of the offer are documented in writing.

I've read this advice somewhere. However, I'm unable to recall the specific source. Regardless, it is essential to remember that salary negotiation is a dialogue, not a monologue. Effective communication, respect, and finding a mutually beneficial solution are critical to a successful negotiation process.

XIII. Consultant Contact with Candidate Contact After Acceptance is Periodic until Start Date

Plan to stay in touch periodically with the Candidate for various reasons, but primarily to make sure that nothing has changed, the family is onboard, the Candidate has resigned or will be leaving soon, there is no counteroffer, and relocation, if necessary, is being managed. Everything else relative to the change in jobs has been addressed.

XIV. Consultant Contacts with Client Quarterly after Assessing Performance of Candidate Filling Completed Assignment

Many search firms stay in touch with their clients only if they are trying to acquire more business. In your case, you will reach your client every three months for the first year on average to learn how well your Candidate is doing and whether they are on target to meet or exceed expectations. Communicate similarly with your Candidate.

XV. Placement Satisfaction is Guaranteed for One Year After Reporting to Assignment

Typically, if a Candidate is terminated within one year after starting, many firms will redo the search at no cost to the client other than expenses. Some firms offer less, but it varies firm by firm.

BEFORE YOU GO...

Please take a moment to spread the word and help other recruiters.

By sharing your honest opinion of this book and a little about your own experience, you'll show new readers where they can find the resource they're looking for – and you'll help me create more of the resources you want to see in the future too.

Thank you so much for your support. Your feedback is important

CONCLUSION

By implementing a thoughtful and organized strategy for sourcing, identifying, and recruiting passive, top-ranked Candidates, you can significantly simplify your job. Throughout this book, we have provided you with a methodology to conduct a search and a series of action steps to help you build a dynamic referral database that leads to the identification and recruitment of exceptional Candidates.

Reflecting on my 35-year career in executive search, I realize that true success was not measured solely by the number of searches won or closed or the revenue earned. What truly stood out were the heartfelt expressions of gratitude from the Candidates I placed, who appreciated my persistent support and encouragement, and the appreciation from clients, who praised my professional representation of their businesses and the quality of the Candidates recruited. Their feedback indicated that my empathetic and determined approach made a significant difference for all parties involved.

Over time, calls from executives I placed and messages from former clients inspired me to write this book. Although I left the search industry with a sense of sadness, many urged me to share my Search Methodology and style with other recruiters, essentially "cloning" myself. Most Candidates and clients believed that my process offered the most consistent, comprehensive, and communicative executive search experience.

The satisfaction of positively impacting the lives of clients that I worked with and Candidates placed became a driving force throughout my career. This required a comprehensive approach, including consulting with clients, conducting thorough research, making strategic cold calls, expanding my network of Sources, and engaging with Prospects and Candidates from previous searches. Consistently following my proven methodology by following each step precisely led me to repeatedly identify the perfect Candidate fit.

By adapting your search approach and utilizing my Search Methodology, you can work smarter and enjoy the success you deserve throughout your career.

Get ready to embark on an exciting hunt using this tried-and-true framework!

If you found this book valuable, please take a moment to leave a review on Amazon. Your feedback is incredibly valuable and contributes to the creation of even better tools and resources in the future. Thank you!

APPENDIX

Following is the bullet point Search Methodology presented to clients (without the explanatory opening paragraphs) that breaks down the thorough, step-by-step process we will follow for each search assignment. This assures circumventing missed steps that could derail a search midstream or, at minimum, allow an opportunity to be lost. Each bullet point below is augmented within Chapters 1 through 5.

SEARCH METHODOLOGY

*In this **Client Acceptance Phase**, the search firm gains an understanding of their client company, the key personalities of the leadership team, and a definition - aka position description - of the job assignment. The position description includes performance standards, responsibilities, organizational authority, critical problems to be solved, and probable growth paths for the successful Candidate. Time is devoted to developing a definition of the Candidate, including preferred education, personality characteristics, and ideal fit with superiors, peers, and subordinates. Additional information sought is the delineation of the bare minimum requirements of any Candidate as well as the makeup of the ideal Candidate, a summary of the compensation package, a definition of target corporations as well as compa-*

nies to stay away from, and written documentation of the above and confir-mation in a letter to the client.

A. CLIENT ACCEPTANCE PHASE

I. Definition of Corporate Structure, Products & Services: Objectives and Related Plans

II. Definition of Organization: Key Personalities Surrounding the Assignment, including Incumbent

III. Definition of Job Assignment: Performance Standard, Responsibilities, Organization Authority, Key Problems to be Solved, and Future Growth Path for Successful Candidate

IV. Definition of Candidate: Education, Personality, Charisma, Characteristics, Fit with Superiors, Peers, and Subordinates

V. Delineation of Critical (Must Have) Job & Candidate Characteristics Priority List

VI. Definition of Optimum (Have Done) Professional Background: College to Present

VII. Definition of Compensation Package: Base, Bonus, Deferred Compensation, and Stock Options

VIII. Definition of Target Corporations: Corporate Personality, Priority Definition, Listing of "Out-of-Bounds" Corporations

IX. Acceptance of Assignment

X. Confirming Letter to Client

XI. Documentation of Complete Specification: Search Specification

XII. Review of Write-up with Client

*In the **Research Phase**, an expanded list of target companies is created, including finding appropriate Candidates and Sources in related national associations, gathering a list of previous references from associated searches, and putting together a competitive or priority rating of target companies.*

The next step involves developing the organizational structures of target corporations and researching individuals who have recently departed from these companies. Potential Candidates and Sources are identified, and back-

ground summaries are compiled. Compensation ranges for similar job titles and scope of responsibility are examined.

Following this, the identified sources are contacted according to the priority listing. Even if these individuals are not interested, their career goals and plans are still explored. This information is valuable for potential future opportunities and for utilizing them as a resource to identify other Candidates for the assignment.

After two to three weeks of outreach and generating interest from interested individuals, detailed profiles of individual Prospects, including their professional histories and priorities, are prepared. These profiles are then discussed with the client company.

B. RESEARCH PHASE

I. Listing of Target Corporations
II. Listing of Related National Associations and Key Individuals
III. Listing of Known Proven Sources in the Industry
IV. Comparative/Priority Rating of Target Corporations
V. Development of Organization Structures of Key Target Corporations
VI. Listing of Sources in the Key Target Corporations
VII. Listing of Corporate Officers Who Recently Left Target Corporations
VIII. Preparation of Priority Source
IX. Preparation of Preliminary Prospect List and Comparison to Job Write-up
X. Define Target Organizational Level for Each Corporation/Define Corporate Compensation Policies
XI. Contact Sources per Priority Listing
XII. Contact Prospects per Priority Listing
XIII. Contact Associations for Additional Source Development
XIV. Prepare Individual Prospects Detailed Professional History and Source Comments

XV.Comparisons of Prospect Data to Search Specification
XVI.Prepare Prospect Priority List

*In the **Prospect Development Phase**, the search firm reaches out to all viable Prospects on the priority list. In cases involving retained search firms, the client company may often not be disclosed this early, as the search could be aimed at replacing a current employee. Instead, the focus is on discussing the position, its potential for growth, and the overall opportunity. If the Prospect expresses interest, the search firm would perform an introductory interview over the phone and gather essential information, including how they would match up against the Must Haves.*

During these calls, the recruiter would also capture the Prospect's skills and background, probe for critical alignment with the client's needs, explore areas of suspected weakness, and - if the Prospect is on target - define a few additional details of the assignment.

The Prospects are then evaluated against each other, considering their strengths and weaknesses based on the search specifications. Subsequently, the most viable Prospects are interviewed a second time over the phone with the intent of probing much deeper and broader into their background. The strongest of these Prospects will be interviewed by you in person and are moved into the "Candidate" category. Preparations are made to inform Prospects who did not meet the minimum search requirements.

C. PROSPECT DEVELOPMENT PHASE

I. Contact with Prospects per Priority List
II. Brief Definition of Client, Assignment, and Position Responsibilities (Client is often not Identified)
III. Define Complete Details of the Professional History of the Prospect. Emphasis on Current Responsibilities, Achievements, and Problems
IV. Prepare Prospect History Summary
V. Probe Details of Critical Factors of Assignment

VI. Explore Areas of Suspected Weakness

VII. Define Additional Details of the Assignment if Prospect is on Target

VIII. Comparison to Search Specification

IX. Development of Additional Prospects and Sources

X. Tentative Arrangements for Personal Meeting or Sign-off

XI. Repeat Prospect Development to Assure Broad Industry Coverage

XII. Comparison of Individual Prospects to each other and Search Specification

XIII. Prepare Prospect Strength/Weakness Lists

XIV. Prepare Arrangements for Prospect Meetings and Candidate Development Phase

XV. Prepare Sign-off Letter to Prospects not Meeting Total Search Requirements

*For the **Candidate Development Phase**, the search firm sets up face-to-face meetings with all qualified Prospects, now elevated to Candidate.*

During the interviews, in addition to finishing gathering background infor-mation, you'll observe and note their degree of interest, enthusiasm, eye contact, and other detail you could only pick up in person. You should be able to determine by now whether or not this Candidate is on target and whether you both wish to move forward. If so, the search firm will further discuss the client's identity, organization, and environment, as well as whether the Candidate's needs align with that of the client.

Sometimes, a confidentiality agreement might need to be signed before naming the client and sharing confidential information.

After your in-person meeting with the Candidate, the client would receive a Candidate letter, a detailed analysis of the career history of each Candidate in the running. From a professional career perspective, this detailed personal profile includes summaries of performance responsibilities, accomplishments, failures, relevant company details, and compensation history. Being well-acquainted with the client company, the search firm would provide their expertise in assessing the compatibility of the Candidate's charisma with the client, explore potential areas of concern, and evaluate how well they align with the essential qualifications for the position.

D. CANDIDATE DEVELOPMENT PHASE

I. Personal Meetings with Qualified Prospects
II. Detail Analysis of Professional Profile - College to Present, Plus Develop Reference Listing: Total Organization Analysis, Responsibilities, and Performance, Accomplishments/Failures, Compensation History
III. Personal Detail Profile
IV. Compare Charisma Match with Client
V. Explore Details of Suspect Areas of Concern and Critical Requirements
VI. Decision: Candidate, Sign-off or Hold in Abeyance
VII. Discuss Details of Client Assignment, Organization, and Environment without Identification of Client
VIII. Obtain Expression of Interest in Client Assignment
IX. Identify the Client. This is Held Until the Candidate is Fully Qualified for Both Personal and Professional Needs and Express Interest in Further Exploring Assignment
X. Discuss Details of Client Assignment, Environment, and Personalities
XI. Obtain a Schedule of Candidate Availability for the Arrangement of Future Meetings with the Client
XII. Preparation of Documentation Presenting Details of Professional and Personal History to the Client
XIII. Preparation of Candidate Comparative Analysis to Client

*Communication with the client during the **Assignment Completion Phase** is ongoing to compare each presented Candidate soon after each face-to-face first interview. In consultation with the client, the decision would be made to continue with a Candidate, to sign them off, or hold them in abeyance for the time being. Once the client has expressed interest in any Candidate, detailed* *reference checks are made (with the Candidate's knowledge). The results of these reference checks are then discussed with the client, including questionable factors that arise during these inquiries.*

Then, assume the client decides to act on the leading Candidate. Compensation offers are discussed with the client, and the decision is made to have the search firm or the client offer the Candidate the position. After acceptance, the search firm will periodically contact the Candidate and remain in contact until the start date. The recruiter then maintains, at minimum, quarterly contact with the client to assess the placed Candidate's performance and engagement. Most search firms offer a placement satisfaction guarantee for one year after the Candidate reports to the assignment, which rarely occurs; if so, the recruiter may need to redo the search.

E. ASSIGNMENT COMPLETION PHASE

I. Meeting with Client – Review and Analysis of Candidates with Consultant Recommendation
II. Establish Dates for the Arrangement of a Meeting between the Client and the Candidate
III. Contact the Candidate to Arrange the Time and Location of the Meeting
IV. Confirmation of Client-Candidate Meeting
V. First/Multiple Meetings
VI. Client Interest Expressed. Detail Reference Check Made with Understanding of Candidate. This is Done in the Majority of Cases to Protect the Security of the Candidate's Current Assignment
VII. Critique with Both Client and Candidate of Details of Interest and Questionable Factors
VIII. Client Meeting/Decision to Take Action on First Candidate of Interest
IX.Discussion of Compensation Offer with Client
X. Client Offer to Candidate
XI. Candidate Contact with Consultant
XII. Candidate Acceptance Direct to Client

XIII. Consultant Contact with Candidate after Acceptance is Periodic until Start Date

XIV. Consultant Contact with Client Quarterly after Assessing the Performance of the Candidate Filling Completed Assignment

XV. Placement Satisfaction Guaranteed for One Year After Reporting to Assignment

TWO SAMPLE CANDIDATE LETTERS TO CLIENTS

Names, dates, and companies are redacted to maintain confidentiality

Personal and Confidential

May 8, ███

███████████

Managing Director
██ Management Partners Ltd.
████████████ New York, NY 10020

Dear ████,

As discussed with you, I met this past week in Atlanta with ███████████ and found her to possess the strategic skills, stature, and credibility we seek in our candidate for the Chief Executive Officer with █████████████. The following summary will augment her attached resume.

Until June of last year, ████ was most recently President of the $520 million division of the $900 million ███████ Corporation based in ██████ She joined the company in 1981 as Finance Manager and, over the next 23 years, assumed roles of increasing responsibility across Finance, Marketing, Research & Development, and General Management.

████ is a senior executive with global experience in all aspects of operations. Her background includes extensive experience within the life sciences and biotech industries. In her most recent role as a Division President at █████████, her business has served industry customers across biotechnology, pharmaceutical, and beverage manufacturing. Her expertise encompasses the areas of consumables and other materials used in diagnostic test kits; instruments used in life science research; the development and manufacture of drugs; water purification systems; and services.

During her 25 years with █████████, her achievements included a 50% improvement in new product sales as a percentage of total revenue through implementing a portfolio management process. She successfully acquired various technology licenses and companies, including purchasing and integrating a chromatography media manufacturer. Additionally, ████ turned around a field service group from an operating loss to more than 10% operating contribution. Further, she created and executed a new distribution strategy that increased ███████ in-market growth rate to four times the market growth rate.

On the personal side, ████ was Boston ██ area and raised in ██████, ████████████, then moved with her family to ██████. Her father was a pianist and later conductor for various orchestras, including the Civic Symphony Orchestra of ██████. Her mother was a cellist with the ███████ Orchestra and a music teacher. ████ has two sisters, one a teacher in England and the other a psychiatrist. ████ husband is an ████ and they reside in █████, ██████████ with their two sons, one a junior in high school and the other in fourth grade.

Upon meeting with █████, I found her an exceptionally bright, energetic, and seasoned executive. She was well-prepared for our meeting, presenting a practical and realistic assessment of the circumstances surrounding recent events at ████████, portraying the business as a viable entity for which she could accelerate growth and create stability within the organization while assuring the best team was in place to assist her in dealing with Wall Street, lenders, and the bankruptcy court.

After spending from ████ through ████ attending in Rome, Italy, ████ completed her Bachelor's degree from ████ University in 1975. She moved with her husband and began her MBA program, later relocating with him to the East Coast to accommodate his career growth, completing her MBA at ████ University in December of 1981.

████ was immediately recruited by ████ as Finance Manager, then was promoted to Controller for the ████ Products Division, and was later requested to take over as Vice President of Marketing for the ████ Division in ████ where she held global strategy and product development responsibility.

She was soon promoted to head a business unit within ████████ business as Vice President, where she reported, plus R&D, marketing, and all sales for North America and Japan. ████ went through a significant reorganization in 1995, including a channel strategy change. Then, ████ was promoted to Vice President, Marketing and R&D for the ████ Products Division, where she headed global marketing, product development, new product launches, and, later, North American sales.

With continued accelerated growth at ████ ████ was moved into a complete P&L assignment as Vice President and General Manager of the $130 million ████ Products Division. This group served the diagnostic kit manufacturing space and the drug discovery and laboratory research markets. She oversaw the development of ████ first stage-gate product development process and, later, managed the complete integration and manufacturing strategy of ████, an ████ business she acquired from ████. At this time, her scope included sales, marketing, and R&D across North America, Europe, and Japan and pilot manufacturing in the US and Europe.

Within two years, ████ was named Vice President and General Manager for the ████ Division, retaining P&L for this $125 million integrated business serving life sciences, pharmaceutical, and OEM ████ manufacturers. Products included ████ instruments, services, and consumables. She turned around the services business from a loss position and established distribution deals with firms such as ████ elected a Corporate Officer and a member of the Corporate Executive Committee in ████.

In ████, ████ reorganized once again with the formation of two separate divisions. One was Life Sciences, reformed by melding ████ and various acquisitions. The other was the ████ Division, the ████ Division, formed from the melding of three divisions. While the culture of the business needed to be fixed, and the marketing and sales groups needed to be aligned, ████ determined that this space presented the most opportunity.

With her success, ████ was chosen to assume the role of President of this ████ Division, reporting to ████ CEO. She was chartered with achieving double-digit growth in this newly established business unit with combined revenues of $340 million. This assignment also positions her to assume ████ role in the future.

While there existed a functional manufacturing area providing matrixed services across both businesses, ████ had direct responsibility for two captive systems plants reporting directly via two Plant Managers, in addition to a Division Human Resources Manager and Vice Presidents of Finance, R&D, Marketing, and Global Field Operations, the latter which had oversight of sales, service, and two custom systems manufacturing facilities.

Through reorganization in ▮▮▮▮, ▮▮▮▮▮▮▮▮▮ was promoted to Chairman & CEO, though he lacked complete Board consensus. In early ▮▮▮▮, the Board lost confidence in Mr. ▮▮▮ partly due to poor communication with the Board relative to his growth strategies; ▮▮▮ expressed equal concern during this period. He was replaced as President & CEO by ▮▮▮▮ brought in by ▮▮▮ and retained the Chairman's title until Mr. ▮▮▮ assumed the post upon Mr. ▮▮▮ retirement.

While not having dealt with negative SEC issues (▮▮▮ was a member of the Corporate Executive Committee and developed SOX policies), bankruptcies, or shareholder lawsuits such as those facing ▮▮▮▮▮, ▮▮▮ is confident of her ability to get her arms around these issues and work through them while maintaining stability and continuing the growth of the business. She has credibility with Wall Street and has had exposure at investor and analyst conferences, presenting her newly-repositioned ▮▮▮▮▮▮▮ business as a ▮▮▮▮▮ healthcare entity.

Additionally, when ▮▮▮▮▮ was away for extended periods, ▮▮▮ was, effectively, his voice.

▮▮▮ has experienced great success at ▮▮▮▮ over more than 20 years, and with the CEO role essentially blocked, she elected to depart. Soon after, she has sat on multiple Boards, including a current role as an Advisory Board member for ▮▮▮▮▮▮▮▮▮▮▮▮▮ Division, and has performed consulting assignments as she selectively considers her options.

At the time we contacted ▮▮▮, she was reviewing multiple CEO and COO assignments. However, we have assured her we will conduct no further references or inquiries without her full knowledge and consent. In her most recent assignment, ▮▮▮ earned a base compensation of $312,000, a 55% target bonus, and equity.

Considering ▮▮▮▮▮ active job search, I would like to discuss making arrangements for you to meet with ▮▮▮▮▮▮ your earliest convenience.

Yours very truly,

/s/

William J. Sheweloff
Executive Vice President & Partner

WJS:gh

Enclosure

Personal and Confidential

September 8, ████

████████████████████

Chairman
████, CA ████

Dear ████:

As you know, after our meetings last week with the 3D executive team and you, I met with ████, a ████ corporate Vice President and the General Manager of their $400 million ████ Division. This will provide you with a summary of his personal and professional background.

████ was born and raised in Israel. After his service in the Israeli Air Force from ████ through ████ earning his Bachelor of Science degree from the Institute of Technology in ████ in ████, he immigrated to the United States. He soon began working for ████ in ████. ████ is 46 years of age and lives with his wife, 17-year-old son, and 14-year-old daughter in ████, ████.

On a personal basis, ████ is an accomplished strategist, a driver of growth, change, and performance excellence. I found him to be forward-thinking, disciplined, and high-energy, focused with an interactive and motivational leadership style. He is assertive, confident, yet approachable and personable, and appears accustomed to and effective in high-profile executive roles. His demeanor fosters confidence and trust, and he seems to have irreproachable integrity and ethics.

████ has made solid and progressive contributions during the past 22 years as ████ grew from an entrepreneurial $78 million to today's $3.2 billion revenue. He is a member of the global leadership team and has been a corporate officer since ████. In addition to holding project management, sales, marketing, and new product development roles, he ran global corporate research and development operations. He later managed businesses in Europe, Asia, and the United States with total profit and loss responsibility. He has led engineering/high-tech operations, packaging and consumer-type businesses, and industrial manufacturing units. During his operational career, his organizations have been as large as his present $400 million in revenues, and he held responsibility for a maximum of 27 manufacturing facilities and over 2,400 employees across 46 countries. ████ holds 11 U.S. patents and negotiated and concluded 22 M&A deals representing over $200 million in revenues. Additionally, he initiated significant cost savings, grew EBITDA, started value-based pricing strategies, produced a rapid turn-around of money-loosing businesses, and increased revenues and market share.

████ is a $3.2 billion, publicly traded, global corporation and is considered a leading business with operations in 46 countries, 115 manufacturing facilities, and 18,000+ employees. Since ████, ████ has been Vice President and General Manager of the ████ Division, based in ████, ████. He reports to ████, President & Chief Executive Officer. He is on a peer basis to four other vice presidents and general managers of different product areas: ████, ████, ████ and ████. ████ holds full P&L accountability and decision-making authority for his autonomous strategic business unit. She has all functional positions reporting including, but not limited to, a CFO, vice presidents of North America, Europe, and Asia Pacific, JV and subsidiary president and general manager, vice presidents of global manufacturing and RD&E, directors of global marketing, supply chain, information systems, performance improvement, and human resources, and a business unit counsel.

Considered a division president and managing all operational aspects, ████ business generates $400 million in annual sales, conducts business in 46 countries, has 13 manufacturing facilities, and over 2,400 employees. He increased operating profits by over 15% across six consecutive quarters while delivering 19% EBITA improvement, up from a 15% decline before assuming responsibility while dramatically reducing SG&A and manufacturing expenditures. He improved yields, ROA, and inventory turns, consummated three M&A deals while managing their full integration, initiated new channel strategies, and built, trained, and managed his executive team.

Based in Hong Kong from ████, ████ was Vice President & Chief Operating Officer over all ████████ operating divisions across Asia Pacific. He had full profit & loss responsibility for $330 million in revenues for the business with 27 manufacturing facilities and over 2100 employees. Managing a 12-person team, he directed all operations, initiated organizational changes, managed business development efforts, and upgraded the information technologies within his region.

████ increased EBITDA by 40% over three years while increasing new sales by 20% and reducing operating costs. He hastened growth throughout China by partnering and establishing a joint venture with the Chinese government, fostering two M&A deals, and further expanding business into Malaysia, Australia, New Zealand, and Taiwan. He also merged the ████ division of ████████ and reformatted the new business into eight separate P&L units within his region.

Prior, from ████ through ████, ████ was Vice President and General Manager for the ████████ Division – Europe, based in ████████, ████████. At $80 million in revenues and operations in 11 European countries, this business had previously lost market share and profitability. ████ retained P&L responsibility and managed strategy, operations, financial planning, sales and marketing, and distribution. He reorganized the management team, putting an outstanding group of Country Business Managers in place.

He drove acquisitions, including four direct European competitors, and led the startup of various mid-European operations. Additionally, ████ increased revenues per employee while reducing selling expenses.

Upon joining in ████, ████ was Project Manager for Customer Applications through ████ or the Division. Based in ████, he designed the system, a creative method for utilizing ████ in packaging, and generated $240 million through ████. From ████ through ████, ████ was named Manager, Sales & Marketing for the ████████ Division – Europe, based in ████████, ████████. He grew revenues by over 25% across two years throughout the region and infused a value-added solution mentality across his team.

Relocating to the United States in 1988, ████ was named Director of New Product Development for the ████████████ Division based in Danbury, ████████. He managed all new product development and commercialization strategies in the US. He drove the business' leadership position via state-of-the-art technology and developing leadership by driving the development of proprietary, discriminating products in the rollout of 18 new products in four years, generating over $330 million, and reduced the new product development cycle from 36 to 15 months.

Before returning to ███████ as vice president and general manager, ████ was named Vice President, Technology for global operations at corporate, based in ███████. From ████ through ████, he managed product R&D functions, directed global marketing strategies and product launch campaigns, and oversaw the entire product portfolio, including intellectual property, for each operating division, including total development/commercialization lifecycles. New product introduction increased by 23%, and time-to-market decreased by 30% while he and his team created three new proprietary technology platforms. ████ also made other significant contributions, including saving millions of dollars via new outsourcing solutions.

████ currently earns a base compensation of $250,000, a cash bonus of $200,000, $200,000 in stock per year, which vests over three years, and a company automobile. As discussed with you, ████ has an offer in hand from a prominent VC firm; the package offered to him is quite comprehensive, including a five-year guarantee of employment.

We have assured him that we will conduct limited references with the utmost care and confidentiality. I look forward to hearing from you and discussing ████'s candidacy upon your review of this letter.

Yours very truly,
William J. Sheweloff

Executive Vice President
WJS/cc

SAMPLE POSITION DESCRIPTION SUMMARY TO CLIENT

Names, dates, and companies are redacted to maintain confidentiality

Job Description
Vice President, Asia Pacific

███ Corporation

The Vice President of Asia Pacific reports directly to ███, President of ███ Corporation, and will have an organization of both direct line and matrix with responsibility for ███ Asia Pacific operations with a northern segment in Japan; the central segment referred to as ASEAN including Greater China, India, and Korea; and a southern region of Australia and New Zealand.

The current headquarters for the Vice President of Asia Pacific is located in Singapore, operating as ███ Far East Ltd. Singapore. This office houses the administrative management for the Vice President of Asia Pacific.

This position is responsible for developing and executing the immediate and long-range sales plan and leading the company's Pacific Rim operations with a concentration on building a solid ███ presence and brand in this region. The position will have direct responsibility in direct sales, channel sales, and customer support. He will be responsible for developing business partnerships with various software vendors and hardware manufacturers in Asia Pacific. His leadership role will extend to the matrix responsibility for regional consulting services.

It is noteworthy that ███ Corporaton, in the past four years, acquired a consulting company headquartered in ███. The current Director of Consulting and Services for the region is ███ of the original ███ organization, who has a direct reporting responsibility for the North American Business Unit and this position. It is intended that this position will evolve the strategic role of developing the complete regional team relationships to expand the rate of business revenue growth in the consulting area not only in the locations where this organization is aggressively active, heavily weighted to Australia and New Zealand but build that throughout the region. This position will be measured on its performance in generating direct and channel sales, consulting bookings, and expanding its business base.

It should be mentioned that the consulting business is currently focused on performance management products and middleware consulting services. It is foreseen that a strong business application orientation to embed ███ involvement in its customers' business solutions is the direction of growth for the consulting business, and the business consulting model will be emphasized by the individual filling this role. In addition to the consulting practice, ███, Country Manager Australia, will report to this responsibility to develop revenues in Australia and New Zealand.

Currently, the President of Candle Japan, headquartered in Tokyo, will report directly to this position, responsible for developing sales plans, executing both sales and consulting revenues, and building Candle's presence in Japan. Special emphasis in the hands-on leadership of managing this area will be focused on revenues. Additional emphasis will be placed on developing business partnerships with vendors, hardware manufacturers, and system integrators. Additional offices reporting to this role include Hong Kong, which operates as ████ Far East Limited. Under that same entity, the Korean office in Seoul is a part of Asia Pacific Central.

A further matrixed organization includes the reporting of ████████████ Senior Director of Marketing and Communications for Asia Pacific, who has a direct role to ██████, Vice President of Worldwide Marketing. This position executes strategic marketing plans for accelerated business development within ████ and ████ product lines. This work will be integrated throughout the organization to maximize its effectiveness in accelerating the Asia Pacific revenue growth.

We seek an individual whose heritage is most likely in the Asia Pacific region. The executive will likely have had a position with his education divided between the Asia Pacific and the United States. The person likely will have begun his career in a technological role and today will have a depth of understanding of the enterprise software world. The early professional career may have transitioned from technology into a product marketing or sales management role. During that change in professional life, the individual likely will have joined an American or European corporation and have spent time in an English-speaking country while further developing a leadership position and a full appreciation for the operations of a corporation from a United States headquarters perspective.

Our individual's profile will have been selected in the past several years to be the key individual overseeing the management of sales in a multi-regional segment of the Asia Pacific region, ideally overlapping the same countries of our present involvement. This person will have demonstrated the ability to develop a cohesive team of multi-national, multi-linguistic cultures and create the group such that a company will be viewed as a naturally accepted part of its local environment. The person may have had a similar role in Europe before moving to the Far East.

Ideally, we will find that person as a local national in the Far East, so an expectation of overseas expatriation expense will not exist. At the same time, the individual may be headquartered in the United States, overseeing the Asia Pacific region, and, because of their early heritage, they may be motivated to return closer to their original homeland.

The critical dominating measurement, however, will be the ability to build a cohesive team capable of expanding its effectiveness with counterparts in North America while rapidly growing both revenues and ████ dominance in Asia Pacific.

REFERENCES

Cannon, M. (2023, July 17). *21 recruitment quotes for inspiration & motivation.* TextExpander. https://textexpander.com/blog/recruitment-quotes-for-inspiration-motivation

Greenbaum, K. (2019, January 1). A Proud History The Executive Search Profession and AESC. *Executive Talent, 15,* 4-6. https://www.aesc.org/insights/magazine/article/proud-history-executive-search-profession-and-aesc

World, I. (2023, April 26). Executive Search Recruiters Industry in the US - Market Research Report. *IBISWorld.* https://www.ibisworld.com/united-states/market-research-reports/executive-search-recruiters-industry/

World, I. (2023, July 3). Global HR Services Market: Analysis By Type (General Staffing, Professional Staffing and Executive Search), By Region Size & Forecast with Impact Analysis of COVID-19 and Forecast up to 2028. *Research and Markets,* (July 2023). https://www.researchandmarkets.com/reports/5849372/global-hr-services-market-analysis-type#tag-pos-1

Greenbaum, K. (2023, May 3). The Definitive Guide to Executive Search Firms and Pricing. *The Good Search,* (March 2023). https://tgsus.com/executive-search-blog/executive-search-fees-search-firm-pricing/

Media, H. S. (2023, February 6). 2023 Executive Recruiting State of the Industry Study Part I Report. *Hunt Scanlon Media,* (March 2023). https://huntscanlon.com/2023-state-of-the-industry-study-part-i/

(2023, July 10). *Executive Search Services Industry Profile.* Dun & Bradstreet First Research. https://www.firstresearch.com/industry-research/Executive-Search-Services.html#:~:text=The%20global%20executive%20search%20services,have%20offices%20in%20numerous%20countries.

9 798989 627301